Crack Affected Children

A Teacher's Guide

Teacher as Counselor
Developing the Helping Skills You Need
Jeffrey A. Kottler and Ellen Kottler

Crack-Affected Children
A Teacher's Guide
Mary Bellis Waller

Crack Affected Children

A Teacher's Guide

Mary Bellis Waller

CORWIN PRESS, INC.
A Sage Publications Company
Newbury Park, California

94-760

For information address:

Corwin Press, Inc.
A Sage Publications Company
2455 Teller Road
Newbury Park, California 91320

SAGE Publications Ltd.
6 Bonhill Street
London EC2A 4PU
United Kingdom

SAGE Publications India Pvt. Ltd.
M-32 Market
Greater Kailash I
New Delhi 110 048 India

Printed in the United States of America

Library of Congress Cataloging-in-Publication Data

Waller, Mary Bellis.
    Crack-affected children: a teacher's guide / Mary Bellis Waller.
        p. cm. — (Survival skills for teachers)
    Includes bibliographical references.
    ISBN 0-8039-6051-4
    1. Children of narcotic addicts—United States. 2. Children of narcotic addicts—Education—United States. 3. Crack (Drug)—United States. I. Title. II. Series.
    HV5824.C45W35 1993
    362.4'083—dc20
                                                                      92–43185

93 94 95 96 10 9 8 7 6 5 4 3 2 1

Corwin Press Production Editor: Marie Louise Penchoen

Contents

Preface

In a quiet kindergarten classroom, a pretty, well-dressed 5-year-old girl suddenly leapt shrieking from her chair, charged across the room, and snatched a red block from a little boy. She hit him repeatedly on the head and face with the block and then threw it down. Still screaming, she rushed to a shelf, where she scooped all the toys onto the floor. She clambered over the pile of toys and grabbed a doll from another child. Tossing the doll over her shoulder, she stamped her foot and whirled away from the pursuing teacher aide. She smiled as she eluded the aide.

When caught, she tried to bite the aide. Finally subdued, she screamed intermittently as the aide held her in restraint on the floor. She tried to kick the aide and then tried to smash her head backward into the aide's face.

These events took less than 60 seconds and are not uncommon behavior for this little girl. In fact, there were four more violent episodes that day, requiring constant intervention by the teacher and the aide.

This was my first look at a child affected by maternal use of crack. She has enormous behavioral problems, and she is not unique among the children whose mothers took crack or cocaine during pregnancy. Many of the children are left with serious impairments. Some of these are physical, but most are behavioral and learning problems. Schools are usually unable to address these problems effectively with conventional programs.

Crack became widely available in the mid-1980s, and the oldest crack cohort is now about 7 years old. Because so little is known about the behavior of school-age crack-affected children, there are no programs that will reach and teach those children in schools. The tragedy is that while schools wait for the research to come in before designing programs, a 7-year cohort of children is being lost.

Research to date has been primarily on infants, not on school-age children. One of the primary researchers is Dr. Ira Chasnoff of Northwestern University Medical School in Chicago. He and others have been working with drug-addicted mothers, studying them and their babies. Their research is extensive and valuable, but unfortunately, it does not document work with school-age children.

Why Was This Book Written?

Crack-Affected Children: A Teacher's Guide grew out of my experience described in the first paragraphs—and scores more just like it. I found that this child's teacher had been given no information on handling, to say nothing of teaching, the little girl. The school district had simply sent her a short article describing the effects of crack on the fetus and newborn infant. I also found that the same teacher had two more crack-affected children in her classroom. There were at least 20 others in that school alone, and this was in a medium-sized Midwestern city not considered to have much of a problem with drugs.

I decided to find help for that teacher. Mistakenly, I assumed such help existed. I contacted several large city school systems, asking them to send me any information they had on working with crack-affected children. Most districts had no information at all. Many said they had no drug problems in their districts!

Others admitted they had problems but had been unable to find any information on providing help for the children. So I turned to the literature. Most of it is in medical journals. I found good information on behavior and problems of newborns, but little on toddlers and children who have survived addiction and prenatal exposure to crack. Nothing could be found that pointed the way to effective programming in schools. Nothing guided teachers in the specialized techniques they needed to teach effectively. Further, I could find no information that could help parents and foster parents in raising their crack-affected children. It became clear to me that many of the children of crack are different from other children in such significant ways that conventional parenting and conventional (even if brilliant) teaching can be not only ineffective but downright harmful.

Current legal definitions that allow children to receive special help do not fit many crack-affected children. For example, some common characteristics are shared with learning disabled (LD) children, but many crack-affected children cannot be designated as LD, which would enable them to get special help in smaller classes. Most crack-affected children do not fit into the category of the emotionally disturbed (ED), although some of the behaviors—such as impulsivity, lying, and violence—can be found in both ED and crack-affected children. Because they are not left retarded by parental crack use, they do not fit into categories for the retarded.

The combination of behaviors often seen in crack-affected children does not entitle them to special help or small classes. Instead, many are being labeled attention deficit disorder (ADD) or attention deficit hyperactivity disorder (ADHD). Unfortunately, children with the ADD or ADHD label are simply placed into regular large classes, and the teacher is informed of the diagnosis, but no special help is provided to the teacher or the child.

Most crack- or cocaine-affected children are never diagnosed. They go into and through the schools, some of them wreaking havoc wherever they go. Because of parental denial, lack of any identification systems from birth or through the social services system, or simply ignorance, they will never receive the special help they need in order to function effectively in the world.

We need new legislation that would clearly define the range of behaviors characterizing crack-affected children as well as children suffering from prenatal use of other drugs or alcohol. New legislation could define those children who are easily overstimulated, are hyperactive, and have memory and learning problems as persons entitled to a low-stimulus environment designed to allow them to learn and succeed.

We need a quicker way to test, evaluate, and diagnose children in need of special help, so that the length of the process from referral to placement can be measured in weeks, rather than in years as it is at the present time. Currently, exceptional education referrals commonly take almost a whole school year. Without this change, we will miss our chance to give crack-affected children their chance at a normal life.

It became obvious to me in my research that the only people who have useful and accurate information about school-age crack-affected children are the teachers. They are the people trying to work with affected children in their own classrooms. They are the real experts, if only because nobody else knows how crack-affected kids of school age learn, how they behave socially, and how they develop. The teachers are the experts because their school systems are not providing in-service training help and timely testing and evaluation services to the children, thereby leaving the whole burden on already burdened classroom teachers. I found and interviewed the experts.

After interviewing 63 teachers who had extensive experience with crack-affected children, I assembled a list of techniques and tips they had found to be effective. I discovered that each teacher had learned some things by trial and error, or accident, that worked in teaching, in calming, and in controlling behavior. No one teacher had all the answers. Most had only five or six. But taken together, their experiences and insights were voluminous. These techniques are included in this book, grouped into categories.

I also interviewed 60 other people who had extensive experience with crack-affected children. This group includes social workers, physicians, psychologists, court workers, attorneys, foster parents, adoptive parents, birth parents, custodial relatives, and more teachers. Many of the descriptions of behaviors and some of the calming and teaching techniques came from this group. Additional information on behavior at different ages came from parents and professionals who filled out a questionnaire on their experiences with crack- and cocaine-affected children. Their answers detail experiences with several hundred children. The input from the questionnaires has been very important in understanding the duration of behaviors and problems. Most of the teachers work with children who are older than 3 years and younger than 8, whereas the questionnaires have been returned by people who have experience with all ages, from babies and toddlers to children ranging up to age 18.

It is not my intent to paste another stigmatizing label on children. I believe the term *crack children* should be dropped altogether. Nor do I wish to point an accusatory finger at parents who used drugs—it is a fact that their children are here with us NOW and we need to work with them NOW.

Our best moral response is to identify behaviors—from whatever cause—that can benefit from a low-stimulus, routinized, safe, intervention classroom; create those classrooms for them immediately; and expect the children to thrive enough to leave the unique classrooms after about 2 years. Impaired behavior *can* be overcome or moderated, and learning and normalization *can* be achieved. If we fail with these children, their problems will increase and they can become a substantial burden to society.

* * *

Crack-Affected Children: A Teacher's Guide shows how schools can respond to the crisis of children affected by crack. It provides an outline for programming, teacher training, and classroom environment.

Chapter 1 summarizes the problem of crack and cocaine use and its effects on children, indicates the type of educational setting that is effective with crack-affected children, and looks at the economic and legal factors in the education of children of the crack epidemic.

Chapter 2 describes the physical and behavioral effects of crack and cocaine on the developing fetus and the newborn baby.

Chapter 3 details the physical, learning, and relational effects of prenatal use of crack and cocaine on preschool and school-age children and the results of those effects.

Chapter 4 presents successful teaching techniques and gives examples for each.

Chapter 5 offers specific help teachers can give parents of crack-affected children.

An annotated bibliography of some of the most important research on crack-affected children concludes the book.

MARY BELLIS WALLER

Acknowledgments

I wish to thank all the teachers who welcomed me into their classrooms and shared their wisdom and work with me. They have courage, initiative, hope, energy, ideas, and just plain determination that all children can learn. Their teaching and caring are an inspiration to all those who are struggling to reach the children damaged by drugs. Now I share that collective wisdom with other teachers.

Thanks to the foster parents, social workers, nurses, and others who were generous with their time and knowledge. They share the commitment to helping crack-damaged children learn to learn.

About the Author

Mary Bellis Waller is Clinical Program Coordinator at the University of Wisconsin-Parkside. Her research interests include developing effective programs to reach and teach drug-affected children; using Myers-Briggs Type Inventory information for in-services for experienced teachers to help them broaden their teaching styles; exploring attributional style and self-esteem of delinquents, and how these styles differ from those of successful teens; following up successful teacher education program graduates to discover the reasons for their success; changing teacher education programs to make them more responsive to minority and low-income students; examining perceptions of cooperating teachers; and using simulations such as "Chairperson" to change attitudes on racism, sexism, and the like.

Waller has written a number of articles on the topic of crack-affected children in schools, including pieces appearing in *Educational Leadership* and *People and Education: The Human Side of Schools*.

Who Are Crack-Affected Children?

Crack-affected children are children whose mothers used crack or cocaine during pregnancy, or possibly those whose fathers used crack during the week prior to pregnancy.

Although most of the research, including Dr. Chasnoff's research in Chicago, has been with drug-using mothers and their babies, a recent Washington University study shows that cocaine molecules bond with sperm. The sperm/cocaine research shows that the motility of the sperm is not affected by the piggyback cocaine molecule, but the effects on the fetus are not yet known. However, if cocaine molecules are entering the egg along with the sperm, some children might be affected by paternal drug use in the week prior to conception, and some children might be getting a double dose of crack during their fetal development.

Researchers feel that crack use during the first trimester of pregnancy has the most harmful effects. First-trimester use definitely has documented developmental effects. It is also thought that the more crack used, the worse the effects. *Harm to the developing baby can be done whenever crack is used.*

There are also thousands of affluent teenagers and preteens whose upper-middle-class mothers used cocaine, the yuppie drug of choice a decade ago. They exhibit the same impairments of behavior and learning that the younger crack-affected children show. They too have not been helped to learn the skills and behaviors that will enable them to survive in school. Middle-class upbringing is no help to children with these problems. They are falling farther behind in school, some are in trouble with the law, they have few friends, and they are unprepared for the future.

How Many Children Are Affected?

The federal government in 1989 admitted that 375,000 children were born annually who were affected by prenatal drug and alcohol use. However, these figures are low. By some estimates, 400,000 children are born each year affected by crack or cocaine alone, with the number increasing. Since 1989, research on drug use during pregnancy has been published. One study, of Pinellas County, Florida, indicated that 14% of all pregnant women had used illicit drugs during their pregnancies.

As early as 1982, an Illinois study including city and suburban hospitals showed that crack/cocaine use during pregnancy ranged from 5% to 17% of all deliveries. Recently, the Illinois Department of Children and Family Services reported that newborns born with traces of illicit drugs in their blood increased from under 10 in 1985 to more than 2,500 in 1991. Milwaukee County reported a 1991 rise of 82% in the social service referrals for infants whose mothers used cocaine or crack during pregnancy. One Milwaukee hospital has found that 18% of babies born there between 1988 and 1992 tested positive for cocaine at birth. Blood tests do not determine how many were born to mothers who used crack during pregnancy, but only those born with the drug in their blood, showing use within a few days of the test.

The number of newborns with positive cocaine tests is increasing as new crack markets are opened up by urban drug gangs and rural entrepreneurs. Some experts estimate that unless the drug flow is stopped—either cut off at the source or its use cut off through education—by the year 2000, a full 10% of infants born in the United States will be exposed to crack before birth.

Clearly, there are now only two kinds of schools: those with a crack problem now, and those that will have a crack problem soon!

What Are Crack and Cocaine?

Crack and cocaine are products of the coca leaf that are ingested to produce a euphoric high. Most is produced in Central and South America. They are chemically similar substances and have the same effects on the developing fetus. Crack is a newer, cheaper, more available form of cocaine that is usually smoked rather than inhaled. It produces a stronger and quicker high than cocaine.

Crack also causes a more severe crash or letdown when the drug high wears off. There is some evidence that crack users are hooked into addiction more easily than cocaine users, because of the faster cycle of use-high-crash-depression-use-high-crash. Regular crack users may use it several times in an hour; cocaine users may use cocaine several times a day.

Some forms of crack commonly are injected. This increases the likelihood that users will get AIDS, hepatitis, or other needle-spread diseases. Many crack users also use alcohol heavily, because it mediates the severity of the crash from the high.

Many crack users turn to illegal activities to finance their drug habits. Many adults and teens of both sexes turn to prostitution or a direct trade of sex for crack. This further increases the odds of contracting sexually transmitted diseases. It also increases the likelihood of pregnancy—an addict needing a fix will not stop to use condoms or other contraceptives.

The stereotype of crack users is that they are poor and Black and lawless and urban. That stereotype is false. Although many poor Black city dwellers are indeed hooked on crack, so are many White adults and junior-high age children in rural areas and small towns across the country. Crack has invaded the heartland and can be found in any village or crossroad.

What Is the Optimal Educational Setting?

The optimal setting to begin to educate crack-affected children is an *intervention classroom* set up to meet their special needs, with teachers trained in the techniques outlined in this book. It is important that we learn from the experiences in California at the Salvin Special Education Center (Los Angeles) and elsewhere. Their programs found that crack-affected children needed to be in a specially planned educational environment for about two years. After that, they were able to be mainstreamed into regular classrooms with a minimum of special support or programming.

It has been my experience that all children want to learn and want to get along with others. Crack-affected children have a more difficult time learning by themselves, by simply observing others. They learn more effectively if they are specifically taught academic and social skills. This book will help teachers do that kind of teaching and also will help them assess the progress such children are making in their classrooms.

Many school districts will fail or refuse to provide an intervention classroom environment and will instead place the children into their regular classrooms or their regular exceptional education classrooms. These classrooms are usually rich in environment and teaching styles—which distracts and overstimulates and makes learning very difficult for the crack-affected child. However, there are techniques that can help the regular or special ed classroom teacher work with drug-affected children, even if they are responsible as well for a variety of other children.

Nevertheless, the best possible start for crack-affected children, with their special problems, is an environment created uniquely for them. Schools must be aware, though, that when such children are provided with this environment, the intervention classroom, they must be maintained in it for about two years. As the experiences of the Salvin Center show, this amount of time is necessary before the children can be fully mainstreamed into the regular school flow.

Without an intervention setting, most of these children will become so patterned in ineffective and antisocial behaviors—and so accustomed to failure—that they will be special ed candidates for the remainder of their school years. I fear that without special intervention programs, their special problems—such as sudden mood swings, outbursts of temper, problems understanding cause-and-effect relationships, and difficulty developing conscience—will lead many crack-affected children into serious antisocial behavior and trouble with the law.

Economic Factors

School districts must set up pilot programs to respond to the special needs of crack-affected children. These programs must be evaluated for effectiveness and the children followed into regular classes.

Based on the California experience with special classes, it appears that the costs of two years of intervention classes compared to exceptional education classes would save districts money in the long run. Exceptional education classes have a smaller student-to-teacher ratio, each one sometimes containing as few as four students, and often also have at least one paraprofessional or teacher aide in the classroom. These programs are expensive because of the high staffing costs. The average costs of educating exceptional children are from $5,000 to $10,000 per year per pupil more than educating children in regular classes.

If crack-affected children are placed into the existing structure of exceptional education classes beginning at age 3, without provision for their own unique needs, many will continue in the special ed stream until the end of mandatory education for the handicapped at age 21. Those who are maintained within the exceptional education framework would cost from $80,000 to $160,000 *more* to educate than if they were provided with unique programs for about two years and then mainstreamed. Therefore, it is economically reasonable, even mandatory, to provide appropriate help and then move the children into regular education classes when they have achieved the skills they need.

In the Washington, D.C., area, four therapeutic early-childhood nurseries have found that early intervention in highly structured environments has been successful with crack-affected children. They found that two-thirds of their children can be successfully mainstreamed into first grade. The Port Washington, Wisconsin, school district found that providing a unique intervention classroom was cost-effective, because it was the alternative to institutionalization of two little boys whose behaviors were beyond the abilities of the school to handle. Juvenile institutionalization costs are commonly more than $3,000 per *month*.

Legal Factors

School districts may be loathe to set up classrooms for children identified as drug-affected. They may be concerned, rightfully, with the effects of labeling the children, which could cause them to be shunned by others and could lead to differential treatment leading in turn to lower achievement. They know that blood tests at birth show only which children were exposed immediately before birth, and that blood tests during childhood do not show prenatal drug effects.

School districts are also aware that parents who have used illegal substances that damaged their children will be highly unlikely to come forward and admit to it. And parents may feel that speculation about prior drug use is pointless.

Some children exposed early and often to crack show few or no evidences of that exposure. In contrast, there are some children who exhibit almost the same set of behaviors that crack-affected children do, yet who have not been exposed to any illegal substances in the first trimester of pregnancy. Children labeled attention deficit disorder (ADD) or attention deficit with hyperactivity disorder (ADHD) exhibit many of these behaviors, generally without the touch and gaze aversion characteristic of crack-affected children. But the ADD and ADHD children can benefit from the austerity, structure, and consistency of an intervention classroom and be helped by teachers prepared to work with crack-affected children.

A response is needed to the rising tide of drug-affected children, particularly those children with the set of behaviors associated with prenatal crack or cocaine use. School districts should go ahead and set up intervention classrooms, basing selection entirely on behaviors of the children rather than on any medical or social information regarding prenatal drug use. The selection to the classroom or any intervention program must be responsive to the needs of the child, not any judgment on the parents and their behaviors.

What Are the
Early Effects of Crack?

Effects on the Developing Fetus

Crack and cocaine can have a number of adverse effects on the physical development of the baby if used by a pregnant woman during the first trimester of pregnancy. Crack use later in pregnancy can cause traumatic damage to the child.

Damage to the Nervous System

Although there is also physical damage, which will be discussed later, the damage to the nervous system is potentially the most serious problem.

In the normal nervous system, messages are transmitted from one neuron to another by neurotransmitters or "messenger molecules" that move across the synapses (the short spaces between neurons). After the molecule moves from the excited neuron to the next neuron, activating the second neuron, it returns to the first neuron to wait for the next message.

In crack-affected babies, this normal pattern is disrupted. *Dopamine* is a neurotransmitter that normally moves from its home cell across the synaptic space, sends an electrical signal through the receiver cell, and then returns to its home cell. When babies have been exposed to crack in utero, the neurotransmitters such as dopamine appear to permanently stay on the receiver cell. This means the baby is in a constant state of stimulation, or is hardwired ON. This mimics the effects of crack itself on the nervous system of the adult user. Crack activates the neurons in such a way that the molecule remains with the second neuron, keeping it in a state of constant excitement until the effects of the crack wear off.

Infants affected by prenatal crack use seem to be in a perpetual state of ON, not because of the presence of a drug in their systems but because of a physical change in the way their nervous systems work. Their neurons are activated in such a way that the infants are constantly excited and stimulated but are unable to distinguish among stimuli. They are unable to calm themselves as normal babies do, are easily overwhelmed, and rarely are able to rest.

Prenatal crack use also affects the limbic system, that part of the nervous system that controls emotions and their expression. Although this is evident in infants that do not respond to smiles or frowns, the long-term effects of the impairment of the limbic system are more evident after infancy, as appropriate emotional responses fail to develop. This damage also affects bonding in infancy, which can negatively influence all other relationships throughout the infants' lives.

Malformations of the Genital and Urinary Tracts

Genital and urinary malformations are among the problems occurring in babies whose mothers used crack during the first trimester. Such malformations are more common than in normal children, but most crack-affected children do not have them.

The damage may range from slight visible deformities to serious functional problems, such as blockages or missing parts. Serious malformations may interfere with elimination and require surgery within a few days of birth.

The population of crack-affected children in 1993 is for the most part under age 9. Because there has been no systematic study of the children's development, there is no way of knowing at this time if there are greater genital problems that will appear only when they reach puberty. There may be impairment of fertility or subtle deformations of the reproductive organs.

Failure of Parts of the Brain to Develop

One research study indicates that maternal prenatal crack use is associated with brain lesions in the babies. Scans and autopsies showed holes in the brain in which no brain activity took place.

Strokes and Other Brain Bleeds

Mothers' use of crack during pregnancy does not directly cause retardation in their babies, as alcohol use does, but crack use can cause traumatic events that may harm the babies' brains, impairing intellectual capacity and physical ability.

Crack causes tremendous changes in the users' blood pressure. Because crack travels across the placenta into the babies' bodies, the babies also experience the sudden and severe rise in blood pressure, which can force the fragile blood vessels in the brain to burst or leak, causing brain bleeds or strokes in the baby. The resulting brain damage can cause mental retardation, blindness, cerebral palsy, or any other brain-injury-derived disorder.

This means that a perfectly healthy fetus can be damaged at any time in the pregnancy. For example, a woman who is not a regular drug user begins using crack or cocaine during the seventh or eighth month of pregnancy. The sudden rise in blood pressure can cause her healthy fetus to burst a blood vessel and die or become brain damaged.

Women who used crack during pregnancy reported that they felt their babies struggle inside them whenever they used crack. They reported that sometimes it felt as if the baby was trying to escape, or was strangling, or was having a seizure. In fact, the flood of the drug does cause oxygen deprivation due to constriction of blood vessels, so the baby is indeed strangling. And there is evidence that babies do have seizures and convulsions inside their mothers during drug use.

The drug-using women were remorseful about what they understood *at the time* to be harm to their babies, but they found the drug to be so seductive that most of them were unable to stop using.

Fetal Addiction

Use of addicting drugs such as cocaine, heroin, and alcohol by an addicted mother during pregnancy actually addicts the fetus to the drug, because the drug crosses the placenta from the mother's body into the body of the baby. The baby's body comes to require the drug for its maintenance and comfort.

When the pregnant woman enters treatment or, on her own, stops using the drug, she will suffer withdrawal symptoms, including severe pain, uncontrollable shaking, sweating, very rapid and irregular heartbeat, nausea, vomiting, and sometimes hallucinations, seizures, or convulsions. Her fetus also suffers greatly during this time, and can die or be miscarried in the process.

Early or Premature Birth

Many crack-affected babies are born early or prematurely (prematurity is officially determined by the size of the infant). Regular drug use, even in small doses, can cause early labor, and sometimes drug-using mothers make themselves go into very early labor by taking a large dose of crack, in order to end the pregnancy.

Premature babies and babies born before they are full term in development are more likely to require long hospitalization and expensive and specialized care. Add the special problems of crack-affected infants, such as convulsions, constant repetitive motion, and symptoms of withdrawal, and it could be quite some time before they are large enough or strong enough to go home.

Early and premature babies are more susceptible to sudden infant death syndrome (SIDS). One study found that the sample population of crack-affected infants was 10 times more likely to die in the first year of life than infants not drug-exposed. They also are more likely to suffer from apnea, or interruptions in breathing, especially while sleeping. Many crack-exposed babies are sent home from the hospital attached to a cumbersome monitor with an alarm that sounds when the baby stops breathing. A caregiving family must be trained in infant cardiopulmonary resuscitation (CPR) before taking the baby home, so they will be able to revive the baby if it stops breathing.

Premature and early babies are also more likely than full-term, full-size babies to have problems in school later in their lives.

Low Birthweight

Even when crack-exposed babies are born at full term, they are still more likely to be low-birthweight infants. Low birthweight correlates strongly with higher infant mortality from all causes, including SIDS, and with the tendency to apnea.

Also correlating strongly with low birthweight are learning problems, poor social adjustment, and lack of school success when the children enter school. A higher percentage of low-birthweight babies are learning disabled and emotionally disturbed than are normal-weight babies.

Small Head Circumference

Many crack-exposed infants have smaller head circumferences than normal children. Although low-birthweight and premature infants are more likely to have smaller head circumferences than normal infants, a crack-affected baby of normal size and normal birthweight is still more likely to have a smaller head circumference than its body size would predict.

In a series of medical and developmental studies, small head circumference has been shown to be linked to intelligence, with children having small head circumference on the average also having lower IQs.

Small head circumference is also shown to be linked to learning disabilities, school problems, and social problems. Affected children are more likely to end up in classes for learning-disabled children, falling one year or more behind in school, failing grades, and experiencing disciplinary problems. Such children are more likely than normal children to be loners, to have few friends, and not to be chosen or valued by other children.

Children exposed prenatally to alcohol and who are born with fetal alcohol syndrome (FAS) also are likely to have a small head circumference and to show the same problems associated with this condition.

Effects on the Newborn Baby

Crack effects on the infant are most often noticed when the mother is high on the drug when she enters the hospital to give birth. This is not uncommon, especially when the mother is involved in drugs-for-sex exchanges and pregnancy affects her value in the exchange. Street information tells pregnant women that crack will bring on labor, so they use crack to try to end the pregnancy.

If a baby is born alive from this attempt, it may be so premature or so damaged that it will die. If it is saved from death by intensive and expensive medical intervention, it may be abandoned by its birth mother, whether damaged or not, and spend its life in foster families or as a boarder baby in hospitals or group facilities.

Most of the damage done to a baby occurs during the first trimester of pregnancy, and the fact or effect of prenatal drug use is not discovered until birth, or later. At this time, the mother's admission of prenatal drug use and professional observation of the behavior of the baby can indicate the damage.

Further, if the mother isn't high or showing unusual signs when she enters the hospital, most hospitals do not ask questions about drug use during pregnancy.

There are observable common characteristics of crack-affected babies. Neonatal nurses working in intensive care units with crack-affected infants confirm that the infants are jumpy, trembling, and sensitive, and often have convulsions. Visiting a hospital intensive-care nursery serving crack-affected babies is an unsettling experience, as the tiniest victims are so affected and their behaviors are so distinctive.

Addiction

Just as an adult-user addict suffers during withdrawal, so do the infants suffer who are passively addicted by their mothers' drug or alcohol use. The babies tremble, shake, and thrash about, and are subject to severe convulsions that can cause them to stop breathing or to break their bones. Babies born addicted, to addicted mothers, are also in pain during the process of withdrawal, called neonatal abstinence syndrome (NAS). They must be sedated, but they are still in much greater danger of dying during withdrawal because of the withdrawal trauma than a normal baby is of dying during the first few weeks after birth.

In some cases, the effect of the convulsions is so severe that the constant and repetitive movements can wear the skin off the baby's arms, legs, feet, or head. These movements can continue 22 hours a day and are involuntary.

Caregivers in nurseries experienced in working with crack-affected babies have learned that closely wrapping and swaddling the newborns can keep them from hitting and hurting themselves, and can cut the rate of infection by preventing them from wearing their skin away.

The most severely affected infants must be given drugs to keep them from convulsing and to calm the constant movement, which uses up calories, interferes with feeding, and keeps them agitated and sleepless. Many practitioners in the field have grave reservations about using drugs on babies so grievously afflicted by drugs, as the long-term effects of strong drugs on little bodies already weakened is unknown. However, others believe that the calming effects of sedatives and other drugs can help the babies survive the first few crucial weeks and help them become calm enough to thrive.

Babies born to crack-using mothers may not be born addicted. For instance, if their mothers used crack only during the early weeks of pregnancy and were not themselves hooked into constant and regular use, the babies will not be addicted. Similarly, if the mother used a massive hit of crack to start an early labor, but had not been a regular user before, the baby will not be born addicted.

However, if the mother used crack during the first trimester of pregnancy, there is a strong likelihood that the baby will be damaged by that use and will exhibit symptoms and behaviors similar to those of babies born addicted.

Cerebral Palsy

In a given month in Wisconsin in 1991, a pediatric orthopedist ordered 18 sets of leg braces for babies with cerebral palsy (CP)—of these, 14 sets were for infants damaged by crack use. In the next month, the same pediatric orthopedist ordered braces for 14 more babies with cerebral palsy—this time, 13 sets were for babies affected by their mothers' prenatal crack use. This doctor believed that over the next decade there would be a tremendous rise in the number of babies with CP from brain injuries as a result of crack use.

Babies who return home with drug-using parents are unlikely to be taken to a specialist for a handicapping condition because of the disorganization of the lives of the parents, and because drug users are likely to stay away from official agencies that could provide help to an infant. Almost all the families above whose babies were being fitted for braces were foster or adoptive families.

Why are any crack-affected babies allowed to go home with their drug-using mothers? Most states place a priority on protecting and keeping families together. Only in cases of severe abuse or neglect will the state initiate custody proceedings. Termination of parental rights is a lengthy process, sometimes not completed until the child is 2 or 3 years old. Even when it is accomplished, finding adoptive parents for an older and damaged child of an addict is difficult. Many of the children will spend their entire lives in "temporary" situations.

Constant Catlike Crying

Crack-damaged babies often cry many hours a day, to the dismay of their caregivers. Foster parents describe the crying as "unearthly," "weird," "like an animal," and "sounding like a cat about to fight."

A normal newborn will have a repertory of cries—ranging from a whine, to a tentative cry, to a forlorn wail, and finally to a series of furious bellows, depending on the situation—and each of these cries will use several pitches or tones. A crack-affected baby seems to have only one or two notes, emitting what seems to be a constant and piercing wail, and no distinctions of situation. This means that the infant will sound the same whether just waking up, desperately hungry, wet, or stuck with a pin.

A difference in intensity of the cry may signal the physical state the infant is in, whether rested or exhausted, but not the situation, whether hurt or hungry. This inability to signal what the baby wants or needs is frustrating to the parent or caregiver.

Crack-affected infants are often unable to be comforted, and even if fed, held, changed, or cuddled will continue to wail, adding to the frustration of the caregiver. Healthy, experienced foster parents have reported that the constant, unearthly crying wears them out and discourages them. They reported that the normal babies they have cared for over the years cried sometimes during the night, but could be comforted and quieted to sleep or rest, whereas the crack-affected babies cannot be.

For mothers fighting a drug problem and already having a difficult time coping with life, the addition of a baby who cries constantly, making a strange animal-like sound, is sometimes the last straw. Many crack-affected babies are abused by mothers driven over the edge by their crying.

Extreme Lower Body Stiffness and Extension

Many crack-affected infants are born with their hips and legs stiff and straight, and bent somewhat backward in an arc. Often their toes are pointed, completing the arc shape.

Without therapeutic intervention, the stiffness and extension of hips, legs, and feet can persist and cause ligaments and muscles to grow abnormally or to atrophy. Also, without intervention the infant is unable to go through the developmentally necessary steps of creeping, crawling, and then walking. Very early involvement with physical therapy is necessary to counteract these effects. The parents or caregivers must take the infant through a daily exercise regimen in order to bring the lower body to normal use.

Caregivers report that watching the daily exercises is emotionally very wrenching, as the babies cry and scream from pain as their legs are moved gently each day. The extreme stiffness also makes holding the babies difficult and makes cuddling almost impossible, as they are unable to relax.

Hospitals working with many crack-affected babies have learned that they can prop the babies on their sides and fold them into a Z-shaped position, with pillows propped behind the thighs and in front of the calves to help maintain the shape that will allow the child's muscles and ligaments to develop properly.

Inflexible Body

The legs and hips are the most likely parts of the body to be affected, but the entire body of a crack-affected infant is often stiff and rigid.

The infant's arms are often "frozen" into a W shape, bent at the elbow, hands level with the face and balled into fists, elbows somewhat away from the rib cage. When the infant is thrashing about, the hands or fists can repeatedly hit the baby in the face, causing hurt and alarm, and making it more agitated. The agitation then increases the rate of thrashing and hitting. The baby's neck and upper spine are often rigid, and sometimes bent backward somewhat, completing the arc shape of the stiff hips and legs and tiptoe feet.

The inflexible body can be treated by physical therapy, and daily exercises and therapy given by the caregiver. Some programs have successfully used infant massage along with physical therapy, to act directly on the infant's body to relax it. The most successful of these massage programs have begun with newborns. Some experts believe the massage programs are actually reprogramming the damaged neurological system.

Exaggerated Startle Response

Because of the damage to their nervous systems, crack-affected babies are apparently unable to distinguish between familiar and unfamiliar things, people, and events. All stimuli affect them equally, and strongly. This means that they are surprised or startled very easily.

Imagine yourself at a time when you were very surprised, so surprised that you jumped with fright. Your entire body was involved in the jump, your muscles leaped, your eyes opened wide, your breathing stopped, and you gasped for breath. Your heart pounded. You may have felt helpless and unable to run away or move, and shaky and trembling afterward.

Because of the nervous system damage, crack-affected babies experience that strong response when *anything* happens to them. They jump and startle when a person walks near their isolettes or cribs, when they are touched, when their diapers are changed, when they are picked up even for feeding, when they hear a noise, when a shadow interrupts their light, when a breeze blows across them.

Hyperstartle and Shutdown Defense

Because they are ultrasensitive to sensations, and because all sensations have the same effect on them, crack-affected babies are easily overwhelmed and can become self-stimulating and self-exhausting. They can become startled and overstimulated by hearing a noise, then be so startled by their own jump and startle that they repeat, and repeat.

This hyperstartle response leads to exhaustion, and can lead to a loss of consciousness. The loss of consciousness isn't truly sleep, which comes on gradually in phases. It is instead a defense mechanism that can protect the infant from the overwhelming effects of too much stimulation. The baby simply goes limp and out.

This response is well-documented in the infant studies. I have personally seen it in an otherwise well-adjusted 5-year-old when he was overexcited and overwhelmed by a laser show in his school. Two minutes after the lights went out and the lasers began darting around, he slumped over limply. He was unconscious for about 25 minutes and woke normally as if from sleep.

Attention and Tracking Problems

Even as infants in hospital nurseries, crack-affected babies show differences in attention from normal infants. Where normal babies will look at a person bending over the crib and will look at the face of a person holding and feeding them, crack-affected babies are unable or unwilling to look at anyone. One explanation holds that they fail to watch a caregiver's face because the human face is so complex and stimulating that to focus on it is overwhelming to the infant.

This inability to focus is not limited to the human face. Crack-affected infants seem unable to focus on *anything*. It may be that anything they watch closely becomes overwhelming, or it may be that they lack coordination or bodily control to focus.

Where normal babies are able to track a person or an object moving near them, and follow that thing with their eyes, crack-affected babies begin following but then their gaze wanders off. Again, the cause could be overstimulation or neurological damage that prevents them from tracking.

Nurses in neonatal intensive care and foster parents of crack-affected infants report that the infants' tracking ability and attention are so impaired that it is like working with blind babies, whose eyes move randomly but do not follow anything.

Gaze Aversion

Crack-affected babies seldom make eye contact with their caregivers. The avoidance of eye contact is referred to in the literature as *gaze aversion*. Gaze aversion seriously interferes with bonding. The lack of eye contact is frustrating for the parent or caregiver trying to "fall in love" with the baby in the normal manner of parental bonding.

Crack-affected babies will squirm and struggle to get away from being looked at. They will attempt to close their eyes, but their coordination is poor and they are often unable to accomplish this at will. Because the attempts by adults to make eye contact often occur while the baby is being held, there is the added stimulation of being touched. The combination can lead to the baby's losing consciousness in self-defense.

Touch Aversion

Besides the gaze aversion, crack can cause babies to be over-sensitive to touch. Babies who are touch aversive do not find pleasure in the cuddling normal babies thrive on. This sensitivity is another example of the tendency to become over-stimulated and overwhelmed by stimuli.

Routine caregiving activities—such as being changed, being picked up, being fed, and being dressed—can cause tremendous stress for the infant. Parents who are themselves under stress because of drug problems often return to drug use because of the frustration they feel when their own baby screams at their touch.

Touch is a primary means of communication with and for infants. Crack-affected infants are handicapped in that normal touch can cause them to become frantic, struggle to escape the touch, and sometimes lose consciousness.

Some very early infant intervention programs are working to desensitize affected infants so that they will accept touch. These programs can involve infant massage taught to parents and used daily, brushing the child's bare skin with a very soft brush, and light stroking. The babies still struggle against the touch, but if it is done very carefully it seems to have a beneficial effect in helping the infants become accustomed to being handled.

Lack of Bonding

The bonding process between infant and parent has been described as "falling in love": each seeking to look at the other's face, seeking the loving touch of the other, and communicating by touch, by gaze, and by loving noises. The bonding that occurs between parent and child sets the pattern for all other relationships in the child's life, so it is an important process.

All of the senses are important in the process of bonding. Some studies have shown that mothers and babies recognize each other by smell within a day of birth. Others have shown that a baby recognizes and is comforted by its mother's voice, having heard it in the womb.

The neurological damage that can cause normal stimuli to overwhelm crack-impaired infants often impairs the bonding process. Crack-affected babies are ultrasensitive to touch, to sound, and to stimulation of all the other senses. This causes them to avoid contact with the caregiver, thus thwarting bonding.

The physical therapy techniques—massage, brushing, stroking—described in the section on touch aversion, have been found to help the infant cope with these normal stimuli and thus develop a more normal relationship with the parent or caregiver. Obviously, widespread use of these very early intervention therapeutic techniques should be encouraged, as they hold hope of normalizing the lives of the affected children. However, unless and until laws are changed, most children will not receive the help they need.

In order to get help, children must be identified as in need of it. This identification can come through a parent or other relative, through social service agencies, or through the schools. Unfortunately, parents usually deny drug use, and schools don't see children until age 5 or 6 unless referred earlier through social services. This may be too late to alleviate the effects of lack of bonding as infants.

Most crack-impaired children are not being identified by schools or social service agencies. Many impaired children are either abandoned in the hospital or are being taken home to drug-using households. The children returning home with user parents are not likely to be entered into any early childhood programs or infant intervention programs, because their parents tend to avoid contact with any authorities or service agencies.

Abandoned babies in foster care are most likely to get help in early intervention programs involving physical therapy and massage. However, only a small percentage of crack-impaired infants are placed into foster care. Many of these are moved from emergency to special to short-term to long-term foster homes, and some abandoned babies stay in the hospital as "boarder babies" because of the lack of foster homes.

Sleep Disorders

Parents and caregivers alike report that crack-affected babies do not have normal sleep patterns. Most report the infants seem to need only 3 or 4 hours of sleep in 24. They say the new babies are unable to calm or comfort themselves and they wail and scream during all their waking hours.

New research on the effects of cocaine on the fetus indicates that damage to the nucleus accumbens may be the cause of the sleep problems (and perhaps other problems). The *nucleus accumbens* is the brain structure that governs circadian rhythms—our sleeping, eating, and other patterns. In a normal fetus, the developing nucleus accumbens "tunes" itself to the rhythm of the mother, and sets the baby's internal clock to that of the mother. The research now shows that cocaine disrupts the nucleus accumbens in such a way that it remains chaotic, like a clock that runs randomly. Patterns do not appear. When the fetus is born, it does not establish a rhythm in its life for waking and sleep states, feeding needs, and the like.

A few very weak and premature babies may do a great deal of sleeping and even have to be wakened for feeding, but for the most part, the infants are characterized as very active babies who need very little sleep and who cry during their time awake.

Many foster parents of crack-affected babies in interviews have described listening to a baby scream in the middle of the night in its crib, then picking it up to check if there was a pin sticking it, or some other cause for the screaming. They reported feeling overwhelmed and helpless because their touch and their care caused the baby to cry louder and struggle to get away from them. Their baby cannot be comforted as normal babies can be.

At times the babies will go out of control completely. Because they are unable to comfort themselves, or allow others to comfort them, their own screams and movements become more stimuli to further intensify their agitation and exhaustion until they lose consciousness.

Eating Problems

Eating problems have been reported by many parents and foster parents. The babies seem very unaware of their bodies in general. With regard to food, this means that they often don't remember how to suck or swallow or chew, or are startled when presented with food.

Some foster parents have reported that they must gently stroke the babies' cheeks and lips with a soft cloth after placing milk or food into their mouths. This stroking stimulates the nerves and muscles of the mouth and teaches the babies that lips and cheeks are used to ingest food. The foster parents report that this technique does seem effective, although because the babies have a short memory span, the stroking must be repeated with each feeding for weeks or even months.

Foster families have reported the babies seem afraid of new kinds of food. Because they are so sensitive and resistant to change, any change in food texture or taste or temperature can become an overwhelming and traumatic event. Faced with a slightly lumpy baby food, the infant will cough and spit and choke, scream and struggle, and work itself into a tantrum and exhaustion.

Lack of Physical Coordination

Crack-impaired babies are often clumsy and uncoordinated. Although they are usually very active, their activities are not smooth. For example, with regard to hand-eye coordination, the crack-affected baby is likely to make abrupt gross movements and be unable to focus attention and movement long enough to pick up a small object.

As the child grows, physical coordination continues to be a problem in creeping, crawling, walking, feeding self, or reaching for and grasping objects.

3

Crack-Related Problems of Preschool and School-Age Children

This listing and description of problems common to crack-exposed children is the result of interviews, a review of the medical and therapeutic literature, questionnaire responses, and personal observations. When mothers used crack during pregnancy, damage to children ranged from imperceptible to severe. Some children will have all the problems listed. Other children who were exposed to drugs will have mild problems, or no problems at all. Severity likely depends on how much crack was used and when in the pregnancy. However, all of these problems have been reported frequently by parents, caregivers, and teachers of crack-affected children.

I conducted lengthy interviews, lasting from two hours to a whole day long, with 63 teachers who had experience with crack-affected children over a period of several years. I sought them out to learn what techniques work in teaching such children. They had information on prenatal crack and cocaine use through several means: Some children's school records included the information. Some parents and caregivers had informed the school that crack had been used during pregnancy.

Some children were wards of the state and their records included the information. In some cases, social workers had been called in to deal with suspected abuse and in their investigations found the mother had been using crack all during pregnancy.

These teachers shared with me all their experiences in working with crack-affected children. They told me and showed me what they did to make personal contact with children; to calm and soothe an inconsolable child; to interrupt tantrums and violence; to teach letters, numbers, and words; and to teach sharing and care. I was invited to sit in on their classrooms and watch what they did. All wanted more information, because each felt that she or he wasn't successful enough with the special problems of crack-affected children and wanted to learn more.

I then interviewed 60 more teachers (after the first round of long interviews) experienced with crack- and cocaine-affected children and found agreement among them and with the first group of teachers.

All the teachers clearly understood that their students (about 300 verified crack- and cocaine-affected children ranging from age 2 to 17, with the majority of children ages 4, 5, and 6) were normally intelligent, and that some were gifted. They also understood that the children had unique learning problems and, more pointedly, had very different behavior problems than they had previously seen. Because most were exceptional education teachers, and had been teaching an average of more than 12 years, they had seen a great many extreme behaviors, especially in seriously emotionally disturbed children. Over and over, they stated that the behavior patterns of crack-affected children were as extreme as, and less predictable than, the behaviors of emotionally disturbed children they had taught in the past.

Responses from others—parents, foster parents and other caregivers, social workers, teachers and other school support staff—were gathered by questionnaires asking them to state the number of crack- or cocaine-affected children they had lived or worked with, the ages of those children, and then the behaviors the children commonly exhibited. They reported experiences with more than 250 additional children, ranging from infancy to age 17.

The combination of interviews with 123 teachers and questionnaires from caregivers and other social service and school personnel provided a useful look at long-term problems. Many of the respondents are foster parents or adoptive parents who have lived with the crack- or cocaine-affected children since birth, and who have 5 to 7 years' (or more) involvement with a single child or several children. Their experience indicates that without treatment or intervention, many of the problems reported by teachers persist in early childhood at least until second grade. Those reporting on teenage children affected by prenatal cocaine use report many of the same learning and behavior problems in middle school and high school as those behaviors reported by early childhood teachers.

Dr. Barry Zuckerman, Boston University Medical Professor, at a conference in Madison, Wisconsin, stated in 1992 that the behavior problems teachers reported with crack-affected children were simply the "every-day behaviors of inner city children." My research indicates to the contrary that even when babies are abandoned at birth and adopted by middle-class families as infants, and never raised in a chaotic drug-using family, their distinctive learning and behavior problems exist and persist. Most of the foster and adoptive families responding are clearly middle-class, middle-American families, and they are stable and traditional. Babies taken to their homes are not being raised in inner cities nor among drug users.

Many children born to crack-using mothers are abandoned at birth and left in the hospitals of their birth. A Child Welfare League of America study surveyed the hospitals of five American cities on one day of 1989. They found that on that day alone, 304 babies had been abandoned in the hospital, and at least 69% of these children showed signs of impairment attributed to maternal drug use, particularly cocaine. Abandoned babies are put into foster homes if such homes are available, but in more and more areas, the number of children in need of care exceeds the number of foster homes available.

In many instances, foster parents have reported being given no special information or help on how to work with a crack-affected child or infant. Social service agencies are both overwhelmed and unaware of the special needs of these fragile infants and so are unable to provide the information and support foster families need to help the children. Foster parents have been a very valuable source of information on making emotional contact with crack-affected babies and learning to comfort them and accustom them to touch. They have also been a good source on how behaviors persist over time.

Some of the behaviors are age-limited; for example, it is inappropriate to speak of a 2-month-old baby as speech-delayed. However, when a child is 2 or 3 years old, the development of speech, or of physical coordination, or of walking skills is a benchmark to look at appropriate development. *All* respondents working with children age 5 or older reported that the children didn't show remorse for their harmful acts and didn't develop conscience, as would a normal child.

Drs. Chasnoff and Zuckerman, who have done many of the infant studies, have been quoted as stating that because crack-affected children have normal IQs, they are normal children. My research indicates that the situation is not so simple to judge. The intelligence tests they have administered are on a one-to-one basis with one adult and one child at a time, not group tests. They do not require observation of the children at free play. They do not require the children to choose and organize objects or information. And the children test out across the entire normal range of intelligence.

The teachers I interviewed and the caregivers I questioned agree that the children's intellects are not directly harmed; they exhibit the whole range of human intelligence. However, the children have severe learning and behavior problems. The teachers and parents have found, however, that the children's intelligence can be used effectively in interventions for many of the behavior problems, and for most of the learning problems.

The problem behaviors range the whole spectrum of intensities from very slight to very severe, and include all those presented below. In some children, only some of the behaviors may exist; in many, most of the behaviors are seen. But all of the children need special help if they are to function effectively in the world.

Physical Problems

Hyperactivity

Children impaired by crack are often hyperactive. Their activity levels are excessive, and their movements are rapid, careless, constant, and gross.

The children run around at high speeds, seeking the sensation of movement rather than hurrying to get somewhere. They are so unaware of their bodies that they often fall over their own feet. They bump into furniture or even walls and doors, because they have not noticed where they are going. This activity presents a danger to the child, as he or she can be hurt seriously by crashing into a wall or chair, and to others, who may be hurt in a collision.

Many caregivers have reported that their crack-impaired children are constantly bruised and bandaged from the time they learn to walk and that they do not seem to learn from their experiences.

The hyperactivity extends to "quiet times," such as nap time, sitting in a chair, or sitting on a lap. The child seems unable to keep her body still or relaxed. The legs and arms and head are moving constantly. She squirms to get out, or up, or down, or off. When free again, off she goes, racing and crashing.

Ritalin and other drugs are often tried with crack-affected children, with very mixed results. Many schools have reported that they have found hyperactive children responded well to Ritalin and similar drugs and that the drug calmed them enough to allow them to learn.

The same schools reported that Ritalin sometimes has the opposite result on crack-impaired children, increasing their frantic activity and worsening the inattention. Interestingly, the successes with Ritalin that have come to my attention have involved very young children, who were put on the drug at about age 3. For them it seems to work quite well, and they are able to attend school and participate in most activities. Teachers report serious problems when the drug isn't administered, or wears off during the school day, or when the dosage is changed or a new drug is tried. The children have often had to be removed entirely from their classrooms for behavior problems when the drug was abandoned.

Many professionals have grave doubts about the wisdom of giving more drugs to children already so damaged by drugs. They feel that a nonchemical or behavioral solution is the only ethical response to prenatal drug damage.

Delayed or Awkward Walking

Because of the impaired coordination and the hyperextension and rigidity common at birth, crack-affected children are often late walkers. This can be remediated by early and intensive physical therapy. In effective programs, physical therapists teach the parents how to conduct the therapy daily or several times a day, and the parent and child see the therapist weekly.

If untreated, the stiffness of their legs and hips prevents their timely progression through the normal stages of creeping and crawling that precede normal walking. And when the untreated child does begin to walk, it is usually with stiff legs and on tiptoe, without the opposite-arm swing that characterizes normal walking.

Usually, the weight of the child's body eventually will bring the tiptoe stance down to a heel-toe gait. However, the gait remains rather stiff-legged and awkward. Even when running at full speed, the child's hips and knees and ankles do not flex easily. Turning quickly is difficult for him, as he lacks flexibility. He will often crash into an object or wall because turning requires more flexibility and coordinated separate motions than he is capable of.

Balance often appears to be impaired, but adaptive physical education teachers believe this problem occurs partly because the children have such a difficult time paying attention to anything and partly because their bodies are stiff and rigid.

Random Activity

The lack of focus and pattern in the behavior of crack-affected children is, I believe, indicative of the most serious and longest-lasting problem caused by the drug.

Where normal children will have a point to their play—will have a story to tell about what they are doing, as one researcher stated—crack-affected children will have no patterns. They roam and wander aimlessly in their playrooms and in the classroom. They cannot make sense out of toys, and cannot figure out how to use them. Even if they watch others play with dolls and doll cribs, for example, they do not catch on to the acting out of messages and meanings.

Typically, a crack-impaired child will pull toys or books off shelves, then trip over the pile, toss a few around, kick some more, pick up one or two, then discard them, and continue this pointless meandering. It is as if no object has any meaning to her, as if she cannot connect a doll crib with her own bed, as if she is unable to make connections between any two objects.

The patternlessness extends to other children as well. Because the crack-impaired children seem unable to make connections between things or activities, they are unable to play effectively or normally with other children. They cannot function appropriately in a doll corner, for example, or a block area, or a kitchen, or a painting corner. The random activity seems to indicate that the children have difficulty finding meaning in their activities and their surroundings.

School-age crack-impaired children have difficulty in finding connections between ideas. They have trouble grouping and sorting things. They find it difficult to recognize or identify patterns of things, of ideas, of actions. Teachers report problems with logic, with discerning causes of events like the Civil War, for example, or reasons for things, such as recognizing that bird tracks in the snow mean a bird walked there. One middle-school mathematics teacher has found that eighth graders whose mothers had used cocaine during pregnancy had trouble learning math because math is cumulative and sequential. He feels they will never be able to understand the proofs, logic, and building on previous facts needed for high school math.

Impulsivity and Violence

Crack-affected children characteristically are very impulsive, acting immediately on the flash of an idea. This behavior regularly places them in danger, as they will run into a street on an impulse, without thinking about oncoming cars. In the classroom (and the home), the impulsivity is displayed by the children's sudden grabbing of objects that attract them. It also shows in sudden movements, such as running out the door or across the room.

Sharing becomes problematical, as the impulse to take an attractive toy or book takes precedence over the child's need to have a companion or playmate. The sudden grab of a toy can turn into violence if the toy is not relinquished.

Because their activity is patternless and planless, crack-affected children live in the moment almost exclusively. They find it very difficult to control their impulses, responding immediately and strongly when they have one and doing whatever comes to mind to carry out the impulse.

The violence that results from acting on impulse is not planned out. It is not premeditated. Parents and foster parents interviewed said that crack-affected children didn't develop violent behaviors as they grew older. They reported that violent little children might continue impulsive violence, but that nonviolent little children didn't become violent.

Because their actions seem so illogical, so unkind, so counterproductive, it is difficult to explain those actions based on normal experiences with children. They do not, in fact, make sense. They cannot be logically analyzed. They seem senseless, which they are, and they seem mean, which they may be, or they seem evil, which they are not.

The children themselves are usually unable to explain their actions. When crack-affected children acquire language, they are able to answer questions about their behavior. For example, I asked a 5-year-old why he had run across the classroom and hit another child. He replied, "I had a thought." He could not explain the thought to me. He did say that he was not angry at the other child.

A number of teachers have commented in an embarrassed way, "The only time she smiles is when she's hurting somebody," and, "He gets an evil little smile on his face when he's hurting people." Parents and foster parents have told me they sometimes think the child is possessed. The random nature of the actions, coupled with the inappropriate emotional responses, is unnerving.

Crack-impaired children have a flat affect, or very little in the way of appropriate emotional responses. They commonly frown, or burst into tears or a rage, or grin, with no visible or evident stimulus at all. They do not have reasons for their actions, and their expressions are inappropriate for the situation. Consequently, sometimes with the excitement of fast movement and taking something away from another child, they might grin. They might just as easily frown, or cry, or scream.

Families have reported the necessity of getting rid of pets and of carefully and constantly monitoring babies and younger children, because the crack-affected child otherwise will impulsively attempt to harm pets or younger children.

Teachers have reported that once the classroom is stripped of all extraneous stimuli—pictures, toys, noise, and the like—and the teachers themselves work consistently and specifically with each child to explain each action and each lesson, that the behavior became manageable. This is described in chapter 5.

Sleep Disorders

As we have seen, parents and caregivers report abnormal sleep patterns for crack-affected children. The problem is primarily that the children need very little sleep, that they are awake most of each 24 hours, and that they are very active all the time they are awake. As babies, they cry all night. As toddlers and school-age children, they are up and about at night and can endanger themselves if unsupervised.

Parents find they must remove all dangerous items from the children's rooms, doubly secure windows and window screens, and install locks on the outsides of the bedroom doors. Without these precautions, the children often let themselves out of the house and wander off. Several parents have reported their children wandering in pajamas at 4 a.m. in snow, because their rooms had not been secured with high and inaccessible locks. Other parents have reported destruction of items in the house, or the children playing with dangerous things.

Some doctors prescribe sleeping medication for crack-affected children. This assumes the children need a certain amount of sleep and are not getting it. However, crack-affected children often seem not to need as much sleep as other children or as the adults in their households. If the children are young and must be supervised, parents find it preferable to lock them in their rooms at night. Parents of older children report some children can safely roam around the house at night and be trusted not to harm themselves or go out of doors.

The sleep problems can persist into adolescence. Parents of cocaine-affected teenagers report that the children commonly sleep no more than 3 or 4 hours a night. Generally, lost or little sleep at night has very little effect on the daytime activities of the crack-affected child. Teachers and parents are surprised, but a child who only slept 3 hours during the night stays up and active all the next day in school. She may be crabbier than usual, or have a worse temper, or be a little slower, but she stays awake.

Poor Body Awareness

In general, crack-affected children are not very aware of their physical needs. Besides the problems with sleep, when they will stay up, awake, and active even when exhausted, other body states, such as hunger, pain, and a full bladder, can also go unheeded.

For example, eating is a common problem. The crack-affected child seems unable to understand the cues his body provides about when he's full and when he's hungry. Many parents have reported that sometimes children will eat minimal food for two or three days, and other times they will eat two full meals in an hour. Children have been known to stuff themselves until they throw up, if they are offered food.

One custodial grandmother told her grandson's teachers that late each night she prepares a big pan of oatmeal and sets it on the stove, then arises at 6 a.m. to cook it for the whole family. The pan is large, as there are three adults and three children in the family, and they all eat breakfast together. One morning she awoke to find the pan empty. Thinking she'd forgotten to prepare the breakfast the previous night, she prepared another whole pan, and the family gathered and ate the big breakfast together. Her 4-year-old crack-impaired grandson ate his usual big bowl of oatmeal, then mentioned casually to his grandmother than he had been up early and had eaten his own breakfast alone. He had consumed the entire pan, and eaten another big breakfast two hours later with the family.

The same grandmother remarked that her grandson doesn't seem to know when he's hungry, or when he's tired, or even when he's in pain.

Toilet training depends on a child's awareness of a bodily state. Toilet training of crack-affected children is often very late—many impaired children are coming to school at age 5 still wearing diapers. They simply are unable to understand when their bladders or bowels are full. Then suddenly they have voided and are wet and dirty and upset.

Perhaps no characteristic has raised as many questions as the assertion that the children feel no pain. Some maintain that the children feel the pain, but simply disregard it. There is no evidence that the children are impervious to pain. They feel pain as intensely as other children. However, because of their general lack of awareness of the states of their bodies, their responses to pain can seem inappropriate or minimal.

The impulsivity of crack-affected children often leads them into dangerous or painful actions, and these painful actions are frequently repeated, sometimes within a very short time. I have seen a 4-year-old of normal intelligence climb up on a tall radiator and dive off headfirst to the floor, hurt himself badly, and then repeat the action within 20 minutes. My first response was that he was self-stimulating, that he wanted for some reason to feel pain. However, each time he was just as hurt, just as angry, in just as much pain, *and just as surprised!* He had simply forgotten the results of his thrilling dive, and apparently remembered only the excitement of flying.

Crack-impaired children are seriously handicapped in learning from experience. Teachers who have taught special education classes for 20 years and more, and have taught severely retarded children, report that the retarded children would touch, for example, a bright hot tea kettle once or maybe twice, but learned from the experience and didn't repeat it. These same teachers report that crack-affected children do not learn from these painful experiences. They will sometimes repeat an action daily, each time hurt and surprised at the result.

Impaired Coordination

From infancy on, crack children's coordination is poor. Because there is no known physical damage to the body muscles, ligaments, bones, or nerves from the crack exposure, we must assume that their impaired coordination springs from the same source as their attention problems and body awareness problems. They simply are unable to keep track of their bodies enough to develop good coordination.

Middle-school and high-school teachers who have worked with older children affected by prenatal cocaine use say that the children are notably clumsy. Most of them are placed into adaptive physical education programs, where they have special activities geared to their abilities.

Organized sports are not possible for the children, even though some families send their children to specialists for physical evaluations and the evaluations find no organic damage or impairment.

Adaptive physical education teachers have found problems in balance, in opposite arm/opposite leg walking, balancing, hopping, running, throwing, and batting, and in hand-eye coordination. They have found that the children have trouble following directions unless they are given only one at a time. They have also found that the children have difficulty with simple calisthenics; they do not seem to have the normal flexibility and suppleness.

Physical education teachers who have worked with crack- or cocaine-affected children invariably brought up the fact that their usual teacherly prescription for hyperactive or excessive behavior doesn't work with crack-affected children. The usual treatment is to run off the excess energy. Teachers remarked over and over that the crack-affected children don't wear down, don't get tired, and don't modify their hyperactivity even after hard physical activity.

Teachers have found, however, that as crack-affected children's attention improves, their gross physical coordination and fine hand-eye coordination also improves.

Learning Problems

Language Delays

It is not uncommon for a crack-affected child to enter school at age 3 or 4 and not yet be speaking. Some have no words; some are able to make some demands by pointing and grunting. The children have difficulty learning by themselves, and they are unable to make the emotional contact with an adult that sparks motivation. They often are delayed also in understanding language, not just in speaking.

When language does develop, it is likely to be careless. Enunciation is sloppy, the children seem unable to use words consistently, and gradations of meaning are difficult for them. Some teachers have described their speech as typical of that of some autistic children, who echo words spoken to them but have little or no understanding of their meaning.

Attention Problems

The attention and tracking problems of infancy persist. The children are very easily distracted, and sometimes the child's distraction is imperceptible to an observer.

Even without distractions, however, their attention spans are very short and very erratic. Many crack-affected children are being diagnosed as ADD (attention deficit disorder) or ADHD (attention deficit hyperactivity disorder). This diagnosis is of little help, however, as both conditions are excluded from exceptional education categories in most states. This means that teachers will be told that a child is ADD or ADHD, but the teacher will not receive extra help, nor will the child's presence reduce the class size.

Tasks with serial directions are extremely difficult for crack-affected children, even at ages 7 or 8. Teachers of cocaine-affected older children report difficulty with directions even in the teens. The idea or direction just gets lost, or forgotten, or the child is unable to refocus on the sequence.

Because the children have difficulty distinguishing among stimuli, whatever stimulus is close at hand is more important than any other. Teachers have reported children being distracted by something minor, such as a fly in the classroom, and disregarding a noisy fight taking place near them. They could have been harmed by the fight, but were unable to distinguish important from unimportant stimuli or to realize they should get out of the way.

Memory Problems

Memory is highly idiosyncratic for crack-affected children. All the information seems to go into the child's mind, but the "filing system" appears to be flawed in such a way that the child cannot recall it. This is true of social skills as well as school-work.

Many teachers and parents have told me similar stories about this memory problem. Here is a typical one:

A kindergarten-age child wants to learn to tie her shoelaces. Her teacher teaches her the procedure. Carefully, she repeats the directions and the demonstration. Then the child demonstrates that she's learned to tie her shoelaces. The next day, the child asks the teacher to show her how to tie her shoelaces. The teacher repeats the lesson. The child again demonstrates that she has mastered the task.

The next day, the little girl again can't tie her shoelaces. The technique is retaught. It's retaught every day for another week. Each time, the child shows that she can indeed tie her own shoes without hesitation. She can also describe the action while she's doing it. But she cannot remember it from day to day.

Finally, after consultations with the teacher, the parents give up and buy their daughter shoes that have Velcro closings. All is well for two weeks. One day the teacher sees the child with the Velcro shoes—teaching another child how to tie his shoes!

A similar pattern is shown in learning to read, or learning how to tell time, or learning math facts. The memory is all there, but the retrieval system works only some of the time.

This is particularly frustrating to teachers of older children. We expect older children of normal intelligence to remember things they've been told or been taught, especially when they have demonstrated they know it. This doesn't always happen with crack-affected children.

Lack of Perseverance

Failing to persevere is typical of crack-affected children. Several teachers I interviewed told me they believe the children's attention and memory problems are responsible for this.

I have observed several times that affected children, when instructed to write their names at the top of a page, will write one or two letters and abandon the task. This failure to complete a task becomes more noticeable with more complex or longer tasks, because less is accomplished.

With older children, completing homework is difficult. Writing a whole paragraph as an assignment is a problem, even when the rules for paragraph writing are given at the start of the assignment. Assignments that require understanding a beginning, a middle, and an end are very hard for the crack-impaired child. The child will seem careless and lazy, but in fact is simply unable to recall the assignment and is impaired in understanding the logic of the construction. Just deciding what the main idea is or what the conclusion will be can be overwhelming.

Susceptibility to Stimulus Overload

Even when of school age, crack-affected children are still susceptible to stimulus overload. This means that when too much is happening in the classroom or at home, the child easily goes out of control. The response to overstimulation is generally hyperactivity, although it can be tuning out by turning inward.

The common infant response of losing consciousness has not been reported in the literature as happening beyond infancy. However, as mentioned earlier, I have seen a crack-affected mainstreamed kindergartner, otherwise quite well-adjusted, become unconscious when faced with too much stimulation:

I was visiting his school when a laser show was scheduled in the auditorium. All the children filed in, and the lights went out. The children screamed in delight. Then music began pulsating; the children again squealed. Then laser beams began dancing around the room in time to the music. The children were enchanted.

Two minutes after the show began, the aide came out carrying the little boy. He was completely limp, but breathing regularly. She explained to me that he had "fallen asleep" during the show. I accompanied her to the nurse's room, where she and I sat with him for the 25 minutes it took for him to regain consciousness. He awoke as though from sleep.

Later, I spoke with his teacher and asked about his "falling asleep." She explained that when excited, he generally ran round and round the room, sometimes yelling and sometimes hitting other children randomly. The previous fall there had been a fire in a house across the street from the school. Flames came through the windows and the roof of the house and firetrucks with sirens blaring pulled up and firemen jumped off the trucks to fight the fire. This little boy was excited and ran around the room until, suddenly, he sat down and lost consciousness.

His grandparents report that when things are very exciting at home, he will suddenly "fall asleep." Obviously, this is not sleep. He is so overwhelmed that he puts himself out because he cannot manage the excitement.

This little boy's response is uncommon in older children. The usual response is out-of-control hyperactivity, sometimes accompanied by violence.

Sensitivity to Changes

Universally, caregivers reported that the children were unable to effectively manage changes in their lives. Parents and teachers told me that any change—even a happy one—in an expected routine would send the child out of control. Apparently, the problem is partly the interruption of what is known and safe, and partly the stimulus of the new situation.

Changes in the room decor, a new bulletin board, a bright mobile, or rearrangement of the furniture were listed as causing disruption. Pleasant visits from relatives or friends, even when they went very smoothly and enjoyably, caused the child to be wild and jumpy for the next day or two.

Some children are so sensitive to routine changes that just getting ready to go out for recess is a crisis, changing from one lesson to another is difficult, and putting one book away and taking another one out is tough. The addition of a new child to the classroom can be overwhelming, as can visitors to the room. Field trips and other outings are traumatic.

With older children, moving to a new school or into a new classroom can be very disrupting. Changes in home living environments—such as an adult moving in or moving out, or changing apartments—cause problems that carry over into school.

Even a familiar routine such as eating can be traumatic for the crack-affected child. Foster parents have reported in interviews that their children are violently aversive to new food, sometimes actually seeming afraid of it. New food can be a new taste, a new texture, or a new color. Any changes in food can be disturbing, and the children can respond by having tantrums or becoming hyperactive.

Parents have found, however, that with careful advance explanations and a gradual introduction of the food, the older, verbal children can accommodate the new experience. But it remains a serious problem with younger, nonverbal children and babies.

No Sense of Cause and Effect

Crack-affected children do not seem to understand cause-and-effect relationships or the idea of logical consequences of actions. This characteristic is more obvious as children grow older, when parents and teachers expect logical understanding to develop.

Caregivers have reported that it was impossible for them to play peekaboo with their affected children. When they hid behind their hands, it was as though they were completely gone—their reappearance startled the children rather than delighted them. Their children didn't figure out that the parents would reappear; that moving their hands apart meant their face would be there again; that if their bodies stayed in sight, the parents were still there.

In teaching older children, discipline problems are common. A child who doesn't understand that something will happen if he acts in a certain way cannot be disciplined as most children can. Crack-affected children seem to have a great difficulty understanding that one action causes something else to happen. This can be a failure to grasp, for example, what results when the child pours a glass of orange juice on the kitchen floor: There is a sticky mess that needs to be cleaned up.

Part of the problem is that the children are ruled by impulse and do not take the time to contemplate consequences. However, teachers have reported time and again that the crack-affected children simply are unable to "get" cause and effect. They say that this impairment appears not only in their school lessons but also in discipline, in working with other children, and in socializing.

Another serious learning problem is that the crack-affected children are not equipped to undertake any school assignment asking for analysis, or the reasons or causes of something.

For example, one teacher explained what happened when he asked a middle-school group, including a couple of cocaine-exposed children, what were the causes of the Civil War. The cocaine-exposed children had no clue how to answer the question; they fundamentally didn't understand the concept. One said the war just happened; the other said the war happened because people like to fight. These children had read the same assignments and listened to the same lectures and seen the same videos as the other children. Both had normal range intelligence. But both had difficulty understanding cause-and-effect relationships.

A middle-school math teacher who has taught several cocaine-exposed teens believes they will never be competent in mathematics, because math is sequential and cumulative. He believes that the proofs required in geometry will be impossible for them. Understanding cause and effect is similar to understanding how one thing builds on another, or logically follows from another. The inability to make these connections of reasoning is a serious impairment for many crack-affected children.

No Sense of Limits

As children enter school, they are expected to abide by certain sets of rules. Crack-affected children are often seriously impaired in being able to internalize the rules set out for them.

Teachers report that even when the children themselves are involved in setting up rules for the classroom and for individual conduct, crack-affected children still cannot do the two main tasks: (1) understand a framework of rules in the first place, and (2) abide by the rules once they're made.

Difficulty Making Decisions

Because crack affects the nervous system in such a way as to make all stimuli of equal value, crack deeply affects the ability to make appropriate decisions.

Based on information from the teachers of cocaine-exposed older children, as the children move up through the grades and enter middle school, they are overwhelmed by decision making. They seem to have difficulty deciding the merits of one option over another. They may quickly choose one action over another, but then pick the other, and then become paralyzed in inactivity. If they are asked if they'd like a dime now or a dollar in five minutes, they will choose the dime now.

Again, the problem generally lies in acting on impulse, with no thought to the consequences of a decision.

This problem strongly affects schoolwork. For example, choosing a topic to write about as part of a school assignment on ancient Egypt can be difficult. The crack-affected child most likely will choose something familiar, nearby, and concrete— and unlikely to include anything about ancient Egypt—rather than something appropriate to the assignment.

Another example is in making a decision about the use of time when homework must be done and the child also wants to watch TV or attend a school event. The child's impulsivity affects the decision and the homework is likely to go undone. Although this is also common among "normal" children, the crack-affected child will honestly not understand the consequences of not doing homework or consider them when choosing, say, to watch TV.

Difficulty in Planning and Structuring

As children grow older and self-determination is encouraged, crack-affected children are again at a disadvantage. Because they are unable to distinguish consequences of decisions, and because their attention is impaired, planning ahead in their lives is almost impossible.

Parents and teachers of cocaine-exposed high schoolers and middle schoolers report that the children cannot decide what to do after school; cannot decide or remember to do homework; do not understand the process of planning for their futures; cannot envision a future for themselves; do not understand the concept of a job or work; and generally do not comprehend things in the abstract, such as imagining their futures.

Even when they are assisted in planning their activities or helped to choose courses that would prepare them for employment, they seem unable to understand what this means in reality and have trouble staying with the plans.

Problems of Relationships

Lack of Affect

Crack-affected children characteristically do not show emotions the way normal children do. Many times they have little or no expression on their faces—teachers have referred to their "zombie faces." Even when something happens that spurs them to emphatic physical activity, they do not have any expression. Sometimes, however, they have an expression but it doesn't match their actions.

Teachers say that some children smile only when they are hurting another child. The smile is inappropriate. Some children scream and cry, with no provocation. This, too, is inappropriate.

The inappropriate facial expressions do accurately represent their lack of understanding of emotion and its expression. Crack-affected children really have not developed an early and lasting repertoire of emotions. They have also not developed an understanding of the socially accepted face and body expressions that express the emotions that other people feel. They do not understand their own facial expressions when they see themselves in a mirror, nor do they understand the facial expressions they see on others.

Self-Absorption

Crack-affected children are extremely challenged by trying to understand themselves and the world around them. They cannot make sense out of things, so everything that happens is a surprise and they use a great deal of energy just to survive.

They cannot understand facial expressions, body language, how things work, or how social interactions work. They are so concerned with trying to find meaning that they do not pay much attention to others. Sometimes, of course, they will harm another child taking something away from her. Usually, they are relatively indifferent to others.

Experienced exceptional education teachers have compared this self-absorption to autistic children's lack of awareness of others. The teachers stressed that there are some differences: Crack-affected children acquire language, whereas autistic children often do not; crack-affected children have very short attention spans, whereas autistic children can persevere for hours.

Frequent Lying and Stealing

Without an internal system to limit behavior or follow rules, crack-affected children, as they grow older, frequently lie and steal. These actions are simply the results of acting on impulse and of not understanding cause and effect.

The children are not sneaky or devious. Their lying and stealing is very straightforward. They steal what they want from whoever has it. They lie to get out of trouble. They do not lie to get others in trouble or steal so another is blamed. They simply act on the moment.

They do not understand that lying and stealing are wrong. They have no value judgments about these actions, and do not judge others who also lie and steal. They do not understand issues of right and wrong.

Outbursts of Temper

Even as they grow older, crack-affected children have difficulty controlling their impulses. Their outbursts of temper sometimes grow from having their impulses thwarted. Other times, however, the temper emerges suddenly without any obvious source, and the children are unable to explain what happened.

This is most obvious in interactions with other children. I saw a little girl, in the middle of a calm game of stacking blocks, suddenly knock over the stack, scream in anger, and then hit another little girl she was playing with. Her face was red and was screwed up in fury; her body was tense, her fists were clenched, and her voice was loud and furious. There was no precipitating event: All had been calm and cooperative; nobody had thwarted her; nobody had taken anything from her.

With older school-age children, their temper outbursts can occur on the playground, in the classrooms, or in the corridors of school. There doesn't need to be any precipitating event; the temper suddenly flares. It often disappears as suddenly. Older children are frequently in fights with others, because their outbursts provoke retaliation. Interestingly, teachers report that the crack-affected children aren't themselves quick to retaliate and sometimes seem unaware that they are being provoked.

Sudden Mood Swings

Mood swings are reported frequently in the literature about crack-affected infants. Caregivers report not understanding how a baby can change gears so quickly and so often, from smiles to wails in a matter of minutes. Older crack children can also switch moods from happy to sad to angry to euphoric within minutes. There is not necessarily any trigger to the mood swings; they suddenly emerge from nowhere, as do the outbursts of temper.

I have been given many examples of crack-affected children who will start to laugh (inappropriately) in class, or will suddenly burst into tears, or will shout angrily at the teacher or other children.

A teacher told me of a crack-affected child who, when a child in the class began crying because of a death in his family, just sat and grinned happily at the bereaved child. Later that day, long after the event, he suddenly cried aloud, when nothing sad was happening in the classroom. The child was unable to explain his actions.

The temper and mood swings often make the children social pariahs, as other students try to avoid them in fear for their own safety. As they grow older, other children realize that these behaviors are inappropriate and embarrassing and avoid them for social reasons as well.

Lack of Conscience

Interviews with parents and teachers of children of school age revealed another very serious problem. One of the effects of crack is to inhibit the development of empathy, or of appropriate remorse for a wrong act, and the development of conscience in general.

The children seem unable to understand—or at least internalize—the effects of their actions on others. Even if they are able to describe those effects, they do not feel bad about them or show a normal response of regret for wrong action. Even selfish action undertaken for some future reward is impossible for them. And without this quality, of course, altruism is impossible. The inability to feel remorse or develop conscience seems to be the ultimate result of not understanding cause and effect.

More than anything else, this inability to feel remorse or develop conscience separates crack-affected children from other children. They don't seem to understand that without this quality they will have few friends, if any. Friendships that do occur are rare and usually temporary.

Inappropriate Social Behaviors

During elementary school, crack-affected children exhibit little awareness of appropriate social conduct. They do not understand cause and effect and do not behave as though they do. Other children may or may not spend time with them. Generally, if they are not violent, they will have a playmate or two. By middle school, however, they want to be with other youngsters, and to be like them. They have learned a little by watching others and copying their behaviors, but they have no context in which to place these actions.

Middle-school teachers told me that other middle schoolers are mortified at the verbally and physically inappropriate behaviors of the crack-affected children. For example, crack-affected children may touch other children inappropriately, such as handling their hair or touching their faces or bodies, or may be unaware of concepts of personal space and so draw too physically close for a conversation. This can be perceived as aggressive, threatening, or intimidating by the other children.

Here is one example from a middle school. A student in a short skirt came into the room with a note from the office for the teachers. One student kidded her about the shortness of the skirt. Another said, "Nicole, if that skirt were any shorter, we could see everything you've got."

A cocaine-impaired girl in the class jumped into the kidding conversation with a loud laughing list of the specific parts of Nicole's anatomy that could be seen if the skirt were shorter. Then she got more boisterous and began talking about what could be done with those parts of her anatomy.

She was unable to pick up from the facial expressions of the whole class that they were in agonies of embarrassment because of her. She hadn't been able in her 15 years to internalize any system of understanding what is appropriate and what is not, even though she'd had extra help, a loving family, and caring teachers.

She had not been able to learn social limits. She carried things far past the point of propriety and kidding to the point of vulgarity and offensiveness. And she wasn't even aware that she had erred.

Results of Poor Socialization

Isolation

Most crack-affected children are social isolates. Some are outcasts by age 3 because of their violence. Others are shunned as they grow older because they are self-absorbed and unpredictable. They hurt others, steal, lie, change moods without warning, and let their tempers flare.

Such children embarrass their peers in public because they don't know how to behave. They are unable to learn social poise or expertise by watching or being with others.

Few Friends or Role Models

Because they have few, if any, friends, there is little opportunity for them to be instructed through word or example by companions. And because they are isolated, they have few role models in their sphere of attention.

Resentment

Even with their lack of social abilities, the crack-impaired children realize that they are different, that they do not have friends, and that they drive others away. Because they do not have the skills to change the equation, they often become moody and resentful. Some of them act out their anger violently, hurting others and destroying toys and belongings.

Worsening Social Skills

With fewer and fewer opportunities for gaining social skills as they grow, they fall farther and farther behind others in their age group.

TABLE 3.1 Major Observable Characteristics of Crack-Affected Children

Unfocused, patternless activity	Unable to focus or give pattern to behavior, to "tell themselves a story" about what they're doing, or to recognize connections in what others are doing
No sense of cause and effect	Logical consequences or relationships of actions not understood
Lack of conscience	Problems with lying, stealing; unaware of others' feelings; no empathy
Attention problems	Unable to focus attention on anything for long, even if high interest
Poor language ability	Speech delayed, and then sloppy
Memory problems	Unable to remember reliably things learned; activity, skill, or fact seems to disappear, then can resurface days or weeks later
Hyperactivity	Unable to sit still or stay in one place; move around room, often at high speed
Impulsivity	Unable to control urges; this interferes with learning and with social interactions
Temper tantrums	Sudden and unpredictable tantrums or changes in mood; some children can scream for more than an hour without cessation
Violence	Impulses and mood swings can lead to violence; individuals unable to understand, recognize, or predict this behavior

(Continued)

Table 3.1 (Continued)

Flat affect	Do not show sadness, anger, or joy in appropriate ways; apparently unaffected by normal emotions in others; often appear expressionless
Lack of body awareness	Late walking, and then awkward; sleep disorders; eating disorders, including eating 2 or 3 full meals within an hour, or going without food for a day; feel pain, but do not respond appropriately to it, may continue impulsive pain-producing actions; toilet training problems continuing into school age; impaired coordination
Easily overstimulated	Unable to distinguish importance or strength among stimuli; respond to stimulus overload with hyperactivity or shutting down (losing consciousness); sensitive to changes of any kind
Socially isolated	Self-absorbed; no bonding in infancy, few friends, no intimacy; resentment at isolation
Inappropriate social behavior	Unaware of boundaries of social behavior; unable to learn by watching or listening to others; may take teasing literally and act on it; often too loud or too active; often act out

Reaching and
Teaching Techniques

The previous chapters have set forth the worst-case scenarios and presented the plethora of possible problems that can result from prenatal crack and cocaine use. The massed information is dismal indeed and very discouraging. How can we as educators possibly overcome all these problems? Perhaps we cannot manage *all* solutions, but there are ways to manage a good many. Now we come to the good part!

This chapter presents the teaching techniques that experienced teachers have shared with me. Each example comes from their experiences, and no technique was included unless it was described by more than three teachers during the long interviews. These techniques were specifically cited by these teachers as proven successful with crack-affected children. Furthermore, each technique has been successfully used by teachers of crack-affected children whom I have trained in school districts concerned with the problem of crack.

Basically, these are logical and effective techniques to use with any children who are easily overstimulated, have learning and behavior problems, and are socially isolated. Not only crack-affected children, but also abused, alcohol-affected, and hyperactive children, and children with attention deficit disorder, can be reached and even taught through these techniques.

Demand Attention

Demand the child's attention. Without it, you are unable to teach.

If necessary, focus attention on the task by using touch, by gently guiding the child's head down toward the paper or book, or by carefully moving the child's hand down over the page you are spotlighting.

Because of the child's inability to focus attention himself, you as the teacher must do so for him.

Remember that crack-affected children are very easily overwhelmed and that merely more than one stimulus can overwhelm them. If they are overstimulated, they often respond with hyperactivity, sometimes rushing around the room, sometimes becoming violent. Sometimes the overstimulated and overwhelmed child will run away from you or throw things to distance you from him.

This is a protection mechanism, to distance himself from the source of the stimulation, which is your attempting to focus him on the task.

Remember that the fewer stimuli you use, the more effective you are.

If you are touching the child's hand, do not look directly at the child or talk to the child at the same time. Try to use as few stimuli as possible. Limit yourself to one, if you can. If this is not possible, use only two simultaneously.

Explain the task, without touching the child, and only looking at him indirectly, enough to see if he is listening.

Demonstrate the attention you expect. If you want the child to look at or color on a particular page in a book, show the child that page and how *you* would hold the book open and hold the crayon in your hand.

Look at the child and ask him if he understands what you have described and demonstrated.

If he shows he understands, let him begin while you watch.

If he is still not able to concentrate his attention, gently grasp his head and guide his face downward toward the page. *Do not speak while you are doing this.* Then guide his hand down over the page with your hand.

After you have broken physical contact, then speak to the child, and/or look at him.

Remember, if you look directly into his face, *and* touch him, *and* talk to him at the same time, you may overload his ability to cope and lose your instruction time as well as his trust.

Put Safety First

Safeguard the crack-affected child and other children in your classroom. This is your most important task. Because the behavior of crack-affected children can be so unpredictable, and because some can be violent, you will have greater responsibilities than a teacher of other "normal" or exceptional children.

Inventory your classroom for objects that could become weapons in the hands of an out-of-control child. Remove those objects or collect them in an area near you.

Arrange the classroom so that you are able to see every part of it at all times and are physically able to get to every part quickly.

Train your aide or other classroom helper in safety techniques.

Select work or play groups carefully. Try to keep the crack-affected child in the quietest group. Otherwise, she may become overstimulated and unable to control herself.

Constant monitoring of position and situation and behavior is necessary to a safe classroom.

Alert other teachers whose rooms are nearby that there may be sudden or prolonged noises or flurries of activity in your classroom. Explain the situation. Ask them to cooperate if you need someone to cover for you in an emergency.

Expect to spend some recesses and lunches with the crack-affected child, unless another adult is available to do so in your place. If a child comes to school frantic, if her day has been disrupted, or if she has had temper or mood swings in the classroom that day, or episodes of violence or hyperactivity, she will not be able to readily cope with the noisy playground or lunchroom. These informal settings are full of stimuli, which might overwhelm an already overloaded youngster.

Expect sudden mood swings. Crack-affected children can change moods in a matter of seconds.

Expect temper outbursts with no provocation. Be alert for various physical signs of hyperactivity, such as the child suddenly running around the classroom, throwing something, or yelling loudly.

The mood swings are not necessarily related to anything real in your classroom, or to any action by another child or by you or another adult. School-age children who experience these mood swings or periods of violence are often unable to explain why they happen. They will reply "I don't know" or "I had a bad thought" if they are asked why they did something. These changes are simply a fact of everyday life for some crack-affected children. It is very important for you to understand that they are unable to control them.

Physically Restrain

Learn how to restrain a child. Because crack-affected children are unable to prevent or control their outbursts themselves, it is absolutely necessary for adults in the classroom to be able to safely restrain a child so he does not hurt himself or others.

Several teachers have accomplished miracles by consistently using firm restraint: Children who had whirling episodes of violence daily, or who had four-hour tantrums daily, were held *as long as it takes* until they were calm. They progressively needed to be held for shorter periods at each outbreak, until they eventually would calm down when hugged.

Teachers trained to work with emotionally disturbed children will probably be able to show you how to do a take-down restraint from behind. Basically, it involves wrapping your arms around the child and wrapping his own arms around himself. This restraint also enables you to avoid harm to your face from the child's thrashing head, which can be difficult with older and larger children.

With older and larger children, use a time-out room or a time-out box. When you are physically unable to provide the restraint, safety, and stability of a restraining embrace, a time-out room or box is very effective. The child needs to be restrained, either in an embrace or in an area without stimuli, until he can gain control of himself and calm down.

Restraint and times out are not meant to be punishment. They are specific tools that will allow the child to regain control and remove him from the presence of others while he does so. *Remember that restraining or isolating a child temporarily is supplying the control he is unable to provide for himself. It is not a cruel act; it is an act of mercy.*

Set Routines

Set unvarying routines in the classroom. A major impairment of crack exposure is the inability to structure one's own life. Consequently, setting routines in your classroom and sticking to them is vital in patterning the crack-affected child.

All children thrive on the safety of routines and predictability, but normal children quickly learn to set their own goals and schedules. Crack-impaired children cannot do this. They experience their own lives as chaotic; everything surprises them. They do not, on their own, recognize patterns. They do not make connections of logic for themselves based on past experiences.

Use the same rubric of words to begin the daily routine. It might be that each day starts off with the greeting, "Good morning, class," followed by the response, "Good morning, Mr. Jamison."

Longer routines work better with crack-affected children. If the next part of your classroom morning involves asking the children to report on what happened to them after school yesterday or on the way to school this morning, postpone this kind of free-form response. Instead, add more routine. For example, ask a question that has only two possible answers, such as, "Is it sunny or cloudy this morning?"

The fewer breaks in routine and ritual, the more solid and reassuring your classroom will be for the crack-affected child.

Choices are very difficult for crack-affected children. This is because they are unable to distinguish the value of results of choices. They are unable to discern cause and effect and so cannot judge the effects of the alternative choices. Your student will become more confident if she starts her day with safe patterns of discourse and behavior.

Ask more free-response-type questions or opinion questions of small groups of children rather than the entire class.

When you see that the affected child is comfortable with the start of the day and knows the routine well, you can begin to deviate from the routine and pose more challenging situations, such as choices, opinions, and decisions, in which she is also able to begin to participate.

There are times when she will seem to regress to a state in which any deviation in the routine completely unnerves her. When that happens, bring her close to you for reassurance, and allow her to sit quietly while you expand the routine for the others.

Introduce new information or new lessons in the same way each time. For example, if you read aloud to the class each day, announce that activity in the same way each time, such as, "Put your crayons away, class, because now it is time for our story."

Write yourself a set of introduction cards for each activity and/or subject so that you are cued to use the same words each day for the same activities. After a week or so, the routinized introductions will become part of your life and you won't need the cards any longer.

Transitions are particularly important. When moving from one activity to another, or from one subject to another, explain in advance in the same words that there will soon be a change. When the change time comes, explain what is happening. After the transition has been accomplished, explain what happened. This verbal explanation provides an intellectual accompaniment to the fact of change and will help reassure an affected child.

Use classroom rules. This is an effective way of helping a school-age child with transitions and behavior.

Make a written list of classroom rules. Make sure the rules are familiar to the children and that they can either recite or read the list. Give examples of each rule, and make sure each child can recite or tell examples as well.

Post this list in a prominent place in the classroom. Make a copy of the rule list and put it on the desk of the crack-affected child. For youngsters with some reading ability, this written reminder of expectations is familiar and strengthens the training you are establishing.

Review the list of rules with the affected child several times a day, particularly during or immediately after transitions from one subject or one activity to another.

Demonstrate that the rules are the same for each activity and for each subject. The sameness of the list is reassuring to the child. You are establishing a core of organization and order in the child's experience.

Success was reported by one teacher when her crack-affected student went into a regular classroom for part of each day to work with another teacher. This first-grader was beginning to read and could recognize some of the words on the rule list. He was able to recite the entire list and give an example of each rule. The teacher found that it helped the child and the other teacher when she sent him to the other classroom carrying his rule list along. He was able to review it himself and remind himself of the behaviors and work habits expected of him wherever he was.

Remember That Less Is More

Austerity is the watchword for success in working with crack-impaired children.

Strip down the environment.

Strip down your teaching styles. Understand that the more exciting you try to make your class, the more counterproductive you will be for those children who are impaired by crack exposure.

Carefully examine those techniques that you use daily and the assumptions you make about children's reasoning.

Replan your space, your materials, and your techniques so that you present information in the simplest and least distracting ways.

Reexamine your concepts. Concentrate your planning on concepts that stand alone and require the least amount of previous knowledge.

Plan out the *one* simplest way to present an idea, and be prepared to repeat it as often as necessary.

Think of the *one* manipulative that best illustrates a concept, and use only this one rather than several.

Practice patience.

Forget timetables for student learning. Concentrate on milestones of student learning.

Forget the Rich
Classroom Environment

Imagine the most exciting and stimulating classroom environment possible.

There are bright and interesting pictures and posters on the walls. There are mobiles hanging from the ceiling. The lights are bright. The windows are large and offer a full view of the street, the playground, the landscape, and the distance.

The bookcases are full of inviting and visually appealing books in bright covers.

Toys and equipment and furniture are bright and varied and of many textures, sizes, and colors.

Lively music is playing.

Children in a variety of interesting and vivid clothes are informally grouped in many different configurations. Some are at tables or lab counters working with science equipment, some at easels with paints and charcoal, some at desks. Some are sitting on the soft rug near the bookcase looking through books, and some are building a relief map of the Atlas Mountains in papier mache.

All are involved in many different activities, talking to one another, discovering information and evaluating it. They are enjoying one another's company.

From time to time, each of them speaks to the teacher, who asks them about their work and exploration. The teacher circulates around the room, asking and answering questions.

For many of us, this is an ideal classroom. It is organized to appeal to all the senses, to offer choices, to build skills, and to build community. It is active, involved, respectful, and fun.

It is a minefield for crack-affected children!

Because crack-affected children are so sensitive to stimulation, the rich classroom pictured above would distract them and make learning almost impossible. It would also very likely push them into hyperactivity because of the difficulty they have in coping with stimuli. Everywhere they look, there's something that overloads their circuits. In such a classroom it would be very hard for them to regain control of themselves and calm down.

The ideal classroom environment for crack-affected children is a stripped-down intervention classroom. Start with bare walls and ceilings and empty bulletin boards. Add items that the children themselves have made, and only a few at a time.

Keep the lights as low as possible to still get work done. Low lighting is calming.

Limit the colors and patterns in the classroom. Use plain colors rather than patterns.

Put books and toys away and out of sight. Some teachers have found that tacking plain cloth over the fronts of bookcases and toy shelves works very well. The cloth hangs loosely and lifts freely. This conceals the bright colors and distracting shapes of the items and allows easy access.

Set up the classroom so that you as the teacher will present the toys or equipment or books to the children. It is important to keep the trauma of making choices to a minimum until the children have learned how to choose.

Keep noises to a minimum. Use sound-deadening devices, such as rugs on floor and walls and acoustic ceiling tile. Check the sound transmission in the room and set up a teaching space in the quietest area.

Some teachers reported that softly playing music of a single, uncomplicated instrument has a calming effect on behavior. Two mentioned specifically that Native American flute tapes work best for them. The music is slow, the single flute plays only one note at a time, and there is not a strong rhythmic effect.

Avoid percussion and strong rhythms. They have a disorganizing effect on crack-affected children. The children become caught up in the beat, which tends to escalate into frantic activity.

Set aside one austere part of the room where there are as few distractions and stimuli as possible. Work with the affected children in that prepared area.

Forget Stimulating Teaching

What teaching qualities and abilities are you most proud of?

Many teachers report that they are most proud of their abilities to make learning fun and to vary their teaching styles to meet the diverse learning styles of their students.

Certainly, teacher training promotes careful preparation and mastery of subject matter, but it also stresses motivating students, making high-interest presentations, varying the materials and examples, and varying the presentation styles. Teacher education programs stress developing a repertory of teaching styles so young teachers will reach all the learners in their classrooms.

These hard-earned qualities so valued in normal teaching work against reaching crack-affected children!

Avoid changing teaching styles.

Avoid high-motivation techniques; don't try to be an exciting teacher.

Avoid situations of choices and movement around the room.

Limit the number of transitions in the day.

The inability of crack-affected children to deal with change makes your variety of styles harmful to them. Because they are hampered in making connections between cause and effect, for example, and going from specific to general concepts, your repertoire of styles may confuse them.

If you teach math facts five different ways, they are likely to perceive that they are being taught five different things!

Go Slowly

Slow down. Understand that the learning acquisition of crack-affected children is even more idiosyncratic than that of normal children.

This means that they will learn a fact or skill and be able to demonstrate it one day and not know anything about it the next day. Their memory problems indicate that all the information is probably there, but not retrievable easily. Information and understanding may surface at any time, but probably not when you—or the child—most want it.

Teach One Thing at a Time

To effectively teach crack-affected children, break down the teaching task into a series of subtasks. Present concrete examples and verbally tie them to theories or broader concepts.

Be prepared to repeat a lesson or a concept or a series several times, always teaching each in the same way.

Be prepared to teach the same thing next week or next month. Do not assume that prior mastery means current understanding.

Use One Modality in Teaching

Choose one teaching style that is comfortable for you and stick with it. You might be bored even thinking about this, but in practice you will find it works. Your pleasure with your success will overcome your boredom with the idea.

Certainly, this doesn't mean that in teaching the whole class you will limit yourself to one teaching style. It does mean that when you are working with crack-impaired students you will use one teaching modality consistently with those children.

This might mean that you will give directions to the entire class using a variety of styles and reinforce these directions to small groups of children using a variety of styles. However, you will have best results if you are uniform in the style of your directions given to the individual crack-affected child or small groups of children which include crack-affected children.

Although almost any teaching style can be effective as long as it is consistent and the main teaching mode, some practices can be counterproductive and can interfere with learning.

For example, if you are teaching 5-year-olds and one of your students is a crack-affected child in school for the first time, it is highly unlikely that you can accomplish anything by using higher-order questioning techniques. The child is handicapped in understanding anything about connections and is basically hard-pressed to learn on her own.

Modify and normalize your approach as the child becomes more able to work in small groups and more able to handle diverse stimuli.

Keep Groups *Very* Small

Keep crack-affected students in groups of two or three children. Crack-affected children are distracted and stimulated by people.

Think of a classroom of 22 children. There are 44 darting eyes, 44 scuffling feet, 22 twitchy bodies. There are at least 22 shirts,

22 pairs of pants or skirts, many of them with patterns or different colors. There are spectacular shoelaces and wonderful bright socks and shoes. And the hairbows! And the caps!

Then there are 22 faces with different expressions—smiles, raised eyebrows, thunderous frowns.

There are so many stimuli in a calm and peaceful classroom just from 22 children sitting relatively still that it can easily overload a crack-affected child into hyperactivity.

It is a good experience for a crack-affected child to work with another child, and after a while with a group of other children. Keep in mind the overwhelming stimuli inherent in a group of peers.

Choose the partner or partners carefully. Choose a child with a calm demeanor and a soft voice, and one who knows how to stay on task and understands the classroom rules and can verbalize them.

Plan out a physical location where there will be the fewest stimuli, for the group with crack-affected children. Some teachers report their best success is in setting up a small cooperative group near the teacher, rather than in the middle of the classroom surrounded by other children.

Ensure that the affected child is facing a relatively bare wall or chalkboard. This means that the main stimulus is the peer partner alone, and not a visual extravaganza.

Offer Few Choices

Limit choices in your classroom. Most teachers and children find classrooms exciting if they offer many choices. We commonly offer choices of how to use time, of whom to work with, of which projects to do, of which books to read, and of when to consult with the teacher.

Crack-impaired children are confused by choices. They have difficulty distinguishing important from unimportant stimuli, and they do not understand the consequences of different alternatives.

In the classroom setting they will not be able to evaluate one activity against another. Their impulsivity can hasten a bad choice simply because it is there.

Many classroom teachers reported that crack-affected children not only have great difficulty making sensible or logical choices but that the act of choosing itself—perhaps because they cannot comprehend the consequences—can disorient them. The children, when faced with choosing, become confused, sometimes angry, and often hyperactive, rushing randomly around the classroom.

Limit the Number
of Activities

Crack children are distractible, have attention problems, and are susceptible to overstimulation. Limiting activities will gain you their attention.

Specifically, you might teach four subjects instead of eight, arranging to teach the rest in a different week. Or you might reduce the number of discrete activities within any subject-matter time—instead of three or four different activities to teach and then reinforce a math lesson, for example, prepare one or two activities, and then teach and reteach them, making sure the child has an opportunity to practice and model the concept you are teaching.

Minimize transitions, which can be such a problem for crack-affected children. This has the further advantage of reinforcing facts and concepts and techniques through more repetitions.

Limiting the number of activities and transitions can be very difficult for a classroom teacher who has a crack-affected child integrated into a regular class. The best situation for you and the child in your room will probably be separate planning for the crack-affected child and physical placement near your desk. That will allow you to assign and supervise a more limited work array while the rest of the class is involved with the usual high-interest mix of activities common to classrooms.

Be Specific; Don't Hint

Use direct language. Do not hint. Spell out nonverbal social cues. Because crack-impaired children have probably not developed social functions, they are unable to pick up social cues. They must be told specifically what you want. Evidence of this lack of development is widespread in reports from foster and adoptive parents and teachers. The children seem not to understand what a smile or a frown means and consequently do not respond to them appropriately.

Most teaching in normal circumstances depends a great deal on the children and the teacher sharing a common understanding of what nonverbal social cues mean. Facial expressions, raised eyebrows, eye contact, frowns, voice tone and volume, body language, and distance maintained during conversation are all ways we communicate beyond the words we use.

For a child handicapped in any of the ways a crack-affected child is, social discourse, whether verbal or nonverbal, can be a frustrating and incomprehensible trap. Because the crack-affected child does not have a normal affect and very often cannot pick up on nonverbal cues, he is unaware of what is expected of him and unaware of his effect on others.

For example, in a normal classroom setting, a child's minor misbehavior—such as whispering to another or failing to put a book away when asked—can be dealt with effectively by the teacher using a pointed look ("fixing them with my steel gaze"), or saying the child's name in a stern tone, or frowning.

For a crack-affected child, you must spell out what you want and how the child must respond. If you want him to stop whispering, get his attention by saying his name, then tell him to stop whispering. If there is a specific rules-based discipline system in place in the classroom, state aloud to the child exactly what the penalty will be if he does not stop whispering. When he stops whispering, thank him in a matter-of-fact manner. If he doesn't stop, invoke the penalty.

Your expression and tone of voice have no meaning for him unless and until you explain that your expression is a frown, and that you are frowning for a specific reason. Explain that all people frown when they are angry or upset, and show what that expression looks like.

Teach Facial Expressions and Body Language

Because they are unable to pick up on social cues on their own, common facial expressions and body language must be taught to crack-affected children.

Teach these expressions specifically. Show what a smile looks like while describing it. Tell the child the occasions when people smile. Show the raised eyebrows meaning a question or doubt, and describe them. Give an example or two of when people might raise their eyebrows.

Ask the child to demonstrate a smile, or a frown, or raised eyebrows.

Cut out pictures of people's faces with different expressions. Describe each expression while you are showing it to the child. If necessary, describe and point out each aspect of the expression, such as a frown: the corners of the mouth turned down, and the eyebrows pulled down over the eyes, and the forehead furrowed.

After explaining what the expressions on the people in the pictures mean, have the child pick out the faces illustrating different emotions. For example, choosing all the happy faces, all the angry faces, all the sad faces, all the surprised faces.

Be sure that you explain what the expressions mean: what anger feels like, what happiness feels like. Give examples of what situations could cause those feelings. Have the child explain what would cause him to feel that way for each feeling.

Describe what would cause you to feel that way for each feeling, and model the expression as you describe it.

Give the child a mirror and ask him to practice each expression. Pair him up with another child and have them make expressions at each other and guess what each means. You as the teacher should remain close to the pair if you do this exercise. It is better to start by telling them which expression to practice. Work closely with the pair to be sure they are getting all the aspects of each expression accurately.

Continue with these exercises until the child can recognize these expressions in others and can explain how to appropriately respond to the expressions. For example, if a person frowns in an angry way at the child, will the child approach the frowner? Will the child avoid the frowner? Will the child check his own behavior to see if he is triggering the frown? Have him describe and explain each expression and how he would respond.

Work to make sure the child can recognize and respond to the main repertoire of expressions. We hope that this teaching will enable the crack-affected child to avoid trouble and pain.

Specifically, teach voice expression and projection in the same repetitive way. Be sure you do not ask the child only to emulate your voice or expression. Simply copying an action does not mean the impaired child understands what it means and when and how to use it.

Make an audio tape of inflected voices illustrative of feelings and emotions. Ask the child to demonstrate for you what kind of voice he would use if he felt a certain way. Ask him to describe the feeling and the voice he is using.

Give him an example of a situation and have him show the voice he would use in that situation. Then give another example and do the same thing. Don't give several examples at once; the message might be obscured in the flurry of information.

Specifically, teach body language. Cut out pictures of people with different body positions, such as relaxed in a chair, dozing, in a fighting posture, arms crossed firmly across the chest, off balance, and so on. Describe what these postures could mean.

Have the child tell what the person in each picture is doing and how that person might be feeling. Tell the child to seek clues in the facial expression.

Again, use words to describe the feelings and the evidences of feelings shown by facial expressions, voices, and body language. The impaired child does not have an instinctual knowledge or a self-taught understanding of these clues. Many times the first chance the impaired child has to learn these important qualities is through a teacher taking the time to help.

Appeal to the Intellect

Use words to reach the child's intellect. The emotions are flawed by maternal crack use, but the intellect itself is untouched. Crack-affected children have the full normal range of intelligence. They do have specific learning problems—such as attention and memory difficulties—but the intelligence works, and the child can be reached through the intellect.

To parent and teach normal children we use the emotions to reach their intellects. Think of how you encourage a baby or a young child to master a task. You smile and nod and verbally praise and encourage her. You are speaking with your senses to her emotions.

The literature of teaching is full of examples of motivation, almost all based on an appeal to the emotions, not an appeal only to the intellect or reason. Because maternal crack use has flawed the emotional development of these children, yet left the intellect unaffected, teachers working with crack-impaired children must reverse the usual motivation process. You must reach the emotions through the intellect.

The key to this unusual process is language. Because crack-affected children are very likely to be language-delayed and are also unlikely to learn language well by listening to others, they must specifically be taught language, very directly, very consistently.

Words are the key to their liberation from an existence that lacks meaning, consistency, and pattern. Language reaches the intellect and can help these children understand their world and perhaps themselves.

Do not expect the children to have effective or rich language. The nuances of language picked up by normal children just by listening and watching are hints incomprehensible to the crack-affected children.

Use the language they have to directly and consistently instruct them in more language.

Remember that they, on their own, cannot make connections between experiences as normal children do. They have very serious problems with logic and consequences. Cause and effect is not a concept they are able to learn by themselves, but it is a relationship they can learn and must be taught.

Use language precisely and frequently. Their intellect can be used to develop an awareness of emotions in themselves and in others. Describe and explain everything, including your own expressions, actions, and feelings. Have them describe and explain things as they do them.

Do it again.

Teach Play

Children who do not see patterns or logic in their world will not learn how to play. Play involves acting out some story or idea. Crack-affected children are unable to do this for two possible reasons: They may not have any idea of a story, and they may not have any idea of how to connect a thought to an action.

Teach play specifically. Crack-affected children have difficulty learning from watching others. You must teach them to play directly, using words and demonstrations.

Explain—in words—the object of play and the sequence of activities in play. For example, if the child is in the doll corner, explain that dolls can be babies.

Explain how to hold a baby carefully, and show this as you tell it. Then explain and show how to dress or wrap a baby doll or how to put it in a buggy for a little trip. Explain and show where to go on the little trip. Explain and show what to say when you arrive.

Use this opportunity to reinforce facial expressions and their meanings.

Say and show that you are happy and have a smile when you hold and gently cuddle your baby. Say and show that your baby is sad and crying because she is hungry. Say and show how to hold and feed the doll. Then say and show that the baby is happy—and smiling—now that she is fed.

An older child who wants to be with others but has been isolated socially because of his behavior must be taken step by step through the game.

Explain why people play a game. It is fun to play this game. It is fun to be with others. It is fun to hit the ball. It is fun to win the biggest score. People smile, laugh, and talk to each other when they're having fun. Again, show and tell simultaneously.

Illustrate appropriate facial expressions and body language even to an older child. If the child is still using inappropriate facial expressions and body language even though of school age, it means that he hasn't learned the appropriate ones yet. If you don't teach him, he may never learn.

By the time normal children are a couple of months old, they are able to appropriately respond to others. Consequently, most families and schools are not accustomed to providing such basic and primitive instruction to an older child for something we assume is inborn.

We assume that a child who smiles when he's being hurt is twisted emotionally. In reality, crack-affected children are not able to pick up information on appropriateness by watching others. Appropriate behavior must be specifically taught or they will never learn it.

Teach Social Interactions

Set up a regular schedule of social instruction.

Involve other children in small-group discussion of social interactions. Be specific in describing fully what expressions, what words, and what actions are involved in each social interaction.

Practice common interactions. For example, how does a child greet her principal? Her grandmother? Her neighbor? Another child she doesn't know well? A child she likes a lot?

Practice how to introduce yourself to others. Practice how to ask to join a play group.

Practice asking information or directions.

Practice having a conversation about an event, a situation, or something personal, such as what a child likes or dislikes.

Monitor the small groups. Be sure all the children are participating. Be sure the crack-affected child is listening, is responding, and is doing the appropriate and discussed action.

Suggest to parents or caregivers that they practice these social interactions. Write a list of the situations and the appropriate responses and actions. Help them plan their practice sessions at home. Make sure they understand that the facial expressions, the body language, and the words must be congruent.

Review the process with the child. Ask him what social situation he wants to learn next. Involve him in the listing of things he wants to learn. Check off the tasks with him as they are accomplished.

Require Modeling of Behaviors

Practice new behaviors with the crack-affected child. Demonstrate and explain each behavior to the child.

Require the child to repeat the behavior and describe or tell it at the same time. Repeat this as often as necessary.

A teacher reported spending three weeks of daily practice sessions on how to enter the room at the start of the day, after lunch, and after recess. The child originally charged into and then around the room, sometimes knocking books off desks, sometimes shouting. He wound himself up with his behavior and couldn't calm himself down.

His behavior spurred imitations of this inappropriate behavior by other children. His noise disrupted class work. Admonitions and punishments didn't work. His teacher decided to teach him specifically how to come into the room like the other children.

First, each day she and the child walked slowly into the room while she described in words what they were doing. They walked slowly to his desk while she described the action. She sat him down quietly at his desk, while telling him in words what he was doing. Then she praised him for coming into the room in a good way.

Then, she asked him to say what they were doing as they walked into the room, approached the desk, and sat quietly at the desk. He described the process, some days saying it alone as they walked and some days saying it with the teacher.

After three weeks, he proudly walked into the room alone and sat at his desk. He was able to manage this new skill about two times a day for another week. Then he was able to almost always carry out the new action. Sometimes he needed to describe it quietly to himself. Sometimes he said he just thought it in his head. Either way it worked.

Because he was no longer charging wildly into the room, he was immediately available and attentive for school lessons— and the rest of the class was no longer disrupted.

A Reminder

Remember that the children affected by crack want to be like other children. They want to have friends. They want to "be good." They want to feel the same things other children do, and do the things they do. They want to be able to think and "get" jokes and understand subtle things. They want to play and to enjoy things. They want to succeed in school. They want to succeed socially. They want to understand themselves and the world around them.

With help, they can.

TABLE 4.1 Some Effective Teaching Techniques

Strip down the environment. Simplify the classroom. Reduce all stimuli—visual, audio, physical.

Simplify teaching techniques. Stick with one teaching style. Minimize transitions.

Establish invariable routines. Create an atmosphere of safety and predictability.

Teach language slowly and carefully. Repeat lessons and have the child demonstrate her learning.

Instruct specifically; don't hint. Use words to describe actions and feelings.

Appeal to the intellect and educate the emotions. Use words to do this. Show and tell facial expressions and body language. Teach social cues and give praise and encouragement.

Teach social interactions and play. Use guided practice with other individuals and small groups.

Learn to restrain the child safely. Use time-outs if necessary. Provide the opportunity for self-control to the child and remove him from the original stimuli.

5

Helping Parents of Crack-Affected Children

Most parents or caregivers of crack-affected children do not have access to information that can enable them to reach and help their children: Little information and help is provided to most foster parents. Adoptive parents are often not given accurate information about the history of their child. Birth parents may be busy dealing with their own drug use or recovery.

For many birth parents, the support and help from the school will be their main encouragement to help their children—and through them, to help themselves. Establishing household routines, for example, is necessary for the children's learning and growth and also assists disorganized parents to structure their own lives in a meaningful and efficient way. Practicing social interactions, for another example, is vital for the children and requires the active participation of the parents in an interaction they may not be confident about. It benefits parents and children.

The school will be the main help, resource, and support to such parents. For the good of the children, the things you do in school and the things they do at home should be congruent.

Here are some of the points you can help parents with.

Lower Short-Term Expectations and
Raise Long-Term Expectations

Tell the parents that their child won't necessarily behave or learn the way normal children do. It is unfair to the child to expect him to acquire language and other skills by a certain "normal" time, if he is neurologically unable to do this.

However, a slow start doesn't mean the child won't succeed. The parents must concentrate on developing skills and behaviors in the short run so that the child can learn by himself in the long run.

Understand the Child's Abilities

Be aware that the child's memory problems or irregularities in understanding may obscure her actual abilities. Share your knowledge of the child's skills and abilities with the parents. Inform them about intelligence and other tests and diagnostic approaches. Tell parents whether you believe such tests are accurate or affected by the child's behavior or attention problems.

Be Patient

Most things take a long time with a crack-impaired child. Parents need to understand that they will have to teach and reteach him the same things over and over again. If they have other children, they must understand that they cannot expect the same learning curve from their impaired child.

Do Not Use Violence

Tell parents to not use violence. Do not hit or hurt the child. Do not shout or raise your voice.

The child does not understand cause and effect or patterns of behavior. Hitting or shouting at her only adds to the stimuli she is experiencing; it doesn't make sense to her. Shouting is simply more noise; hitting will only cause pain. Neither will change her behavior. It may only make her more frantic or wild.

Turn Off the TV

Limit TV time. Stress to the parents the importance of not leaving the television on to keep themselves company or because they're used to it. It can cause harm to their child's ability to concentrate and learn. It can overload his ability to handle himself.

TV adds to the noise and conflicting stimuli the child experiences. Keep the home as quiet and peaceful as possible.

Use the time to speak with the child and teach the behaviors he needs to learn.

Remove Distractions
and Stimuli

Remove distractions and extra stimuli from the home, especially from the child's room.

Remove pictures, bright toys and books, wallpaper, and print curtains from the child's room. Paint the walls one color. Use curtains or drapes of the same solid color.

Provide one toy at a time to the child. The fewer stimuli available—colors, shapes, objects, sounds—the more attention she will pay to the parents. When the parents have her attention, they will better be able to teach her.

Some foster parents have reported that they were able to use print crib sheets and toys as long as they were black and white. They found other colors distracted babies and small children, so they eliminated them. Parents must adjust their home environment according to their own child's needs.

Be Consistent

Establish rules and stick with them. Always treat the child the way he has been told he will be treated, by his parents and by his teacher. Any punishments or rewards should be consistent and predictable.

Describe the rules. Describe the consequences of breaking them. If parents must take away a privilege or isolate the child, they must describe in words exactly what they are doing and why.

Parents should be careful about revealing their emotional state to the child. Parents should seem emotionally consistent. Don't yell in frustration. Stay calm. Try to relax. At least *act* calm and relaxed.

The consistency of the parents helps the child see patterns and logic in the world and makes him feel safe.

Establish Routines

Decide the best way to get parents and family up in the morning, and do it the same way each morning.

Decide the best way to get the household organized and get chores done, and do it the same way each day.

Establish a set time for meals. Establish a routine for getting washed up and ready for meals. Stick with it.

Establish a set time for bed and a routine for getting ready for bed. Carry it out the same way each evening.

Family routines are a pattern of sameness and safety to the crack-affected child. The more routinized the day and week, the calmer and more reachable the child will become.

Help Parents Be Teachers

Show parents how to use words to explain everything they are doing. Show and tell is the key to helping their child learn.

The child does not learn well by just watching parents and others do things. She must be specifically taught. She can best be taught in words, accompanied by demonstrations. Tell and show simultaneously.

The parents must explain in words while demonstrating how to do something, and then repeat the entire process. Then they must have the child do the task while explaining in words what she's doing, and then have her repeat the whole thing.

Repeat All Explanations and Demonstrations

The child probably has some memory problems. Parents can help improve his memory by repeating all the things they are showing and telling him. He'll learn best by hearing from the parents and watching them at the same time.

Parents very likely will have to teach some things over and over again. Remember, if it's worth learning, it's worth taking all the time necessary to learn.

Be Firm

Establish rules and discipline for the child, even if it seems she doesn't understand. Parents must work to help the child understand the rules, and they must also try to understand the child's frustration in not being able to understand.

Stick with the discipline. Be firm. Firmness will become a routine that makes the child feel safe.

Know How to Safely Restrain

There will be times when the child will fly out of control and may hurt himself or others. Parents must learn how to restrain him so he can't be hurt. Teachers of the emotionally disturbed have been trained in a safe take-down restraint, which you as a teacher should also know how to do. Teach it to parents.

The child doesn't know how to regain control of himself when he's overstimulated, overwhelmed, or upset. He cannot calm himself down alone. The parent must hold him firmly until he stops struggling and feels safe.

As the parents establish this firm restraint, the child will become calm and relaxed a little more quickly each time. After a while, a gentle hug alone may be able to bring him to calmness.

Teach the Child Social Interactions

Parents must use words to teach the child things that other children learn on their own by watching and listening.

Parents must teach her to share toys and other belongings; to share time with friends or teacher; to share attention; and how and when to say please and thank you. They must teach her how to speak to new people, introduce herself, and talk with others. It's up to parents to give her enough manners to let her have friends.

Use words because the parents' facial expressions, their smiles of approval or frowns of disapproval, don't mean enough to her to change what she's doing on her own.

Parents must also teach facial expressions and body language, describing and showing her what smiles and frowns mean, so she will understand others and what others expect of her.

Teach the Child How to Play

Games are not intrinsically interesting to the crack-affected child. The child may want to be with other children, but not be able to understand what the point of the game is, how to play it, and how to get along with others during the game.

Parents must teach these things because he won't learn them on his own.

Practice the rules and some of the skills of a game with him. Practice hitting or throwing or kicking. Tell the parents to talk about what they're doing while doing it. Then have him do it while the parents describe it to him. Then have him do it while he explains it to them.

Repeat this until the child understands it.

Share the Routines

Parents should work closely with you as the child's teacher in order to share the routines that you and the school have established.

Show them what you are doing each day to reinforce behavior. Show them how you start the day with the child. Encourage them to bring many of those routines into the home so the child has consistency at home and at school.

For example, what do you say to the children about getting washed up for lunch? The parents should start using the same words at home to get their child washed up for breakfast and dinner.

Share the Resources

Share whatever resources the school can provide to help parents.

There may be special resource teachers or counselors who can work with the family in helping the child learn at school and learn socially. If there is an adaptive physical education teacher or a speech therapist working with the child, put the parents in touch with him or her.

Have the family meet with you so they can learn and continue the exercises and speech games from school with the child.

Encourage Parents

Parents must be able to take care of themselves in working with their child. Don't waste any energy on blaming or other distractions from the task at hand. Encourage them.

Their child isn't easy to care for. Help parents learn to conserve their energy. Share with them the techniques in this book. Encourage them to find and join a support group or find a relative or friend to talk to when frustrated or upset.

With the parents' help, their child can learn what he needs to get by in the world. And with their love and care, he can learn how to love and care for others.

Annotated Bibliography

Chasnoff, I. (1991, March). Cocaine use in pregnancy. In *Initiatives III: Risks and Evolving Responses*. Proceedings from conference sponsored by the Illinois Special Education Leadership Institute.

Very detailed exposition of effects of cocaine use prenatally on the developing fetus. Shows low birthweight; small head circumference (associated with small brain size); various congenital anomalies (deformities); likelihood of death in infancy. Also details some continuing problems with organizing self, structuring own activities, language development, and behaving properly when child is toddler. Stresses need for structure, removal of stimuli, and the importance of school.

Chasnoff, I., Burns, K, & Burns, W. (1987). Cocaine use in pregnancy: Perinatal morbidity and mortality. *Neurotoxicology and Teratology, 9*, 291-293.

This study compares infants exposed to cocaine and infants exposed to methadone in utero. There were no differences in neonatal gestational age, birth weight and length, and head circumference between the groups. However, there were significant differences in cocaine users experiencing higher rate of premature labor, precipitous labor, abruptio placentae, fetal monitor abnormality, and fetal meconium staining. Further, cocaine-exposed infants scored significantly lower on the Brazelton Scale in terms of state organization (ability to calm themselves) than did methadone-exposed infants. Further, the cocaine-exposed infants experienced a 15% mortality rate from sudden infant death syndrome (SIDS), whereas the methadone-exposed group experienced a 4% death rate from SIDS. The national incidence of SIDS is 0.5%.

Chasnoff, I., Burns, K., Burns, W., & Schnoll, S. (1986). Prenatal drug exposure: Effects on neonatal and infant growth and development. *Neurobehavioral Toxicology and Teratology, 8,* 357-362.

Data on women addicted to various drugs (not including cocaine) are presented, and developmental assessments of each group of their infants are compared. All groups of drug-exposed infants were smaller on all growth parameters at birth than control babies but caught up by 9 to 12 months. All groups of drug-exposed infants showed abnormal neurobehavior as newborns, but by age 2 were comparable on mental and psychomotor development (measured with the Bayley Scale).

Chasnoff, I., Burns, W., Schnoll, S., & Burns, K. (1985). Cocaine use in pregnancy. *The New England Journal of Medicine, 313*(11), 666-669.

This early study was done to evaluate the effects of the increasing use of cocaine in the United States. It was one of the important signals of effects on early termination of pregnancy as well as abnormal neurologic behavior of the newborns. It compared cocaine-affected infants with infants exposed in utero to other drugs and found no size differences, but significant differences in tremulousness and startle responses for cocaine-exposed babies.

Chasnoff, I., Hunt, C., Kletter, R., & Kaplan, D. (1989). Prenatal cocaine exposure is associated with respiratory pattern abnormalities. *American Journal of Diseases of Children, 143,* 583-587.

This study compares risk to babies born to women using cocaine as compared to women using opiates. Researchers found greater risk (15%) for sudden infant death syndrome (SIDS) for infants born to cocaine-using mothers, compared to previous studies showing 4% risk for infants born to narcotic-using mothers. Cocaine-exposed babies were more likely to experience apnea and other cardiorespiratory problems (38% vs. 6%) than infants exposed to opiates or methadone. It is postulated that this is because of abnormal development of the brainstem and neurotransmitters that control the respiratory system.

Downey, C. (1990, March). Born addicted. *Kiwanis Magazine,* pp. 38-41.

An excellent popular press look at the behaviors of crack-affected children and how those behaviors can overwhelm parents and other caregivers. Does not suggest strategies to help families cope.

Drillien, C., Thomson, A., & Bargoyne, K. (1980). Low-birth-weight children at early school-age: A longitudinal study. *Developmental Medicine & Child Neurology, 22,* 26-47.

Long-term study of low-birthweight children showed high correlation between low birthweight, for whatever cause, and school problems, learning disabilities, illiteracy, failure to complete school, and intelligence. A complete battery of tests ranging from IQ to motor skills to social adjustment was administered at intervals from birth to age 6 or 7. Low-birthweight children were more likely to have experienced postnatal complications. They also had more physical problems, including respiratory and cardiac problems, and more evidence of neurological impairment.

Green, F. (1990, June 13). Officials say schools aren't prepared for first wave of crack babies. *San Diego Union,* pp. A1, A14, A15.

Anecdotal, useful case illustrations of several children who exhibit characteristics of crack exposure. Several interviews, including with Salvin Center administrators, about special Salvin intervention program for crack-affected children.

Gregorchik, L. (1992). The cocaine-exposed children are here. *Phi Delta Kappan, 73*(9), 709-711.

Overview of effects of exposure on young children, and description of program in West Palm Beach, Florida, designed for cocaine-exposed children.

Griffith, D. (1992). Prenatal exposure to cocaine and other drugs: Developmental and educational prognoses. *Phi Delta Kappan, 74*(1), 30-34.

Written by one of the most experienced researchers in the field, this article reports on problems carrying over from infancy to age 3. Griffith shows that intervention and special treatment have worked in bringing exposed children within normal ranges of behavior and development. He suggests keeping behavioral logs so patterns of control loss can be recognized early in the cycle, among other strategies.

Howard, J., Beckwith, L., Rodning, C., & Kropenske, V. (1989). The development of young children of substance-abusing parents: Insights from seven years of intervention and research. *Zero to Three, 9*(5), 8-12.

Focuses on special issues in working with drug-abusing families and disruption of normal relationships between children and parents. Drug-using parents' first commitment is to the drugs, not their children. Outlines difficulties in research on these children and special qualities needed in staffing programs for them. Their studies show a continuum of situations and behaviors and damage; also shows that intervention can help overcome some of the damage caused by drug use and/or disorganized and chaotic families.

Hutchinson, J. (1991, Spring). What crack does to babies. *American Federation of Teachers,* pp. 31-32.

Overview of the physiological damage done to the developing fetus, with an emphasis on the permanent neurological changes caused by crack and cocaine use during the first trimester of pregnancy.

Jorgenson, D., & Wehrmeister, L. (no date). Working with young children prenatally exposed to drugs. *Richmond Unified School District, California.*

Training outline for school staff working with young children exposed to all drugs. Summarizes results of drug exposure and outcomes in behavior, then outlines some strategies for one-to-one work with the affected children. Several reminders not to stereotype the children or their families and instead to treat each child as a unique individual. Good materials for in-service training.

Lewis, K., Bennett, B., & Schmeder, N. (1989). The care of infants menaced by cocaine abuse. *MCN; American Journal of Maternal Child Nursing, 14*, 324-329.

Written by a school nurse, a special ed teacher, and a developmental pediatrician working in an infant intervention program, this is a good review of behaviors common to newborns who are crack-affected. Comparison of studies using Brazelton Neonatal Behavioral Assessment Scale indicates atypical motor responses and poor state control (ability to calm themselves), among other problems. Excellent guide to very early intervention to help infants develop, including extensive chart showing typical problems and intervention responses.

Regan, D., Ehrlich, S., & Finnegan, L. (1987). Infants of drug addicts: At risk for child abuse, neglect, and placement in foster care. *Neurotoxicology and Teratology, 9*, 315-319.

Excellent study of a population of pregnant addicted women, examining the evidence for likelihood of increased child abuse and neglect of children born to drug addicts. They report higher rates of depression in addict mothers, as well as high incidences of domestic abuse and violence and of chaotic living conditions. Subjects were much more likely to have been victims of abuse and molestation than were matched nonaddicted control group. These factors place the addict mothers at high risk for abusive parenting themselves.

Rist, M. (1990, July, No. 9). The shadow children: Preparing for the arrival of crack babies in school. *Research Bulletin, Phi Delta Kappa Center on Evaluation, Development, and Research*, pp. 1-6.

Excellent article summarizing many of the major issues in the field. Summary of statistics on spread of crack, estimates of numbers of children now affected, and predictions of rates of increased use. Summary of infant and fetal effects research. Description of some behaviors common to crack-

affected infants and young children. Recommendations for policy changes to deal with the problem.

Rodning, C., Beckwith, L., & Howard, J. (1989). Prenatal exposure to drugs: Behavioral distortions reflecting CNS impairment? *NeuroToxicology, 10,* 629-634.

This study factored out prenatal drug use from other factors making children at risk, such as poor prenatal care, perinatal complications, and low socioeconomic status. This very important study found that drug-exposed toddlers had lower developmental scores and less representational play than the other high-risk toddlers. The researchers concluded that prenatal drug use compromised the central nervous system. The children were unable to normally initiate, organize, sequence, and follow through on their actions in play settings. Their behavior was patternless and random.

Schneider, J. (1990). Infants exposed to cocaine in utero: Role of the pediatric physical therapist. *Topics in Pediatrics (Lesson 6: In Touch),* pp. 1-11.

Introduction for physical therapists to crack and cocaine effects on infants. Cites research indicating that prenatal cocaine use affects fetal brain neurotransmitters and hence interferes with normal brain development. This is discussed as leading to abnormal brain reorganization and dysfunctional ability to deal with complex environmental demands. Descriptions of infant behavior states, such as sudden fluctuation between extreme states, inability to calm or comfort self, "turning off" when overstimulated and how this interferes with bonding, extreme startle reaction, plus motor control problems and abnormal reflexes. Information on effective handling of infants to respond to their problems, such as positioning of infant, handling, stimulation, feeding, hydrotherapy techniques. Some topics are illustrated with photographs. Information is given on parent education and infant assessment, and several case histories are given.

Schneider, J., Griffith, D., & Chasnoff, I. (1989). Infants exposed to cocaine in utero: Implications for developmental assessment and intervention. *Infants and Young Children, 2*(1), 25-36.

Results of developmental assessments of newborns and young infants. Dysfunctions in motor control were found, as was abnormal state control (ability to calm themselves). Several infant interventions are described to help caregivers cope with feeding, handling, and other frequent contacts with the affected babies. The authors stress that the infants need to be followed into their school years to identify learning disabilities and/or physical or behavioral problems.

Smith, J. (1988). The dangers of prenatal cocaine use. *MCN; American Journal of Maternal Child Nursing, 13,* 174-179.

Overview of cocaine effects on fetal development. Consideration of ethical and legal considerations in working with pregnant drug users. Prevention and early detection of cocaine use advocated. Postpartum care outlined.

Tyler, R. (1992). Prenatal drug exposure: An overview of associated problems and intervention strategies. *Phi Delta Kappan, 73*(9), 705-708.

Pediatrician's overview of effects of prenatal exposure to several kinds of drugs. She emphasizes fetal and infant effects and complications. One section vividly describes environmental influences in a drug-using household. Protective intervention techniques are recommended, such as involving child protection agencies and development of team approaches of school/home/community.

Weber, K. (1991, Summer). Massage for drug exposed infants: An opportunity for integrating the body, mind and soul. *Massage Therapy Journal, 30*(3), 62-64.

Considers infant massage as a very early intervention to normalize the responses of methamphetamine and crack-affected babies. Reports on programs successfully helping drug-affected infants learn to respond more normally to touch, gaze, voice, and face. The techniques used by massage therapists are described and explained. Prognosis is that such intervention can help these children develop more normally.

Weston, D., Ivins, B., Zuckerman, B., Jones, C., & Lopez, R. (1989). Drug exposed babies: Research and clinical issues. *Zero to Three, 9*(5), 1-7.

Overview of policy, health, and economic issues emanating from prenatal drug use. Review of major research studies on the effects on the fetus. Calls for focusing treatment effort and avoiding stereotyping. Calls for using a "risk model" rather than a "deficit model" in addressing issues related to drug-affected children.

Yazigi, R., Odem, R., & Polakoski, K. (1991). Demonstration of specific binding of cocaine to human spermatozoa. *Journal of the American Medical Association, 266*(14), 1956-1959.

First clinical study to report that in lab tests human sperm bind to cocaine. It was found that the cocaine-bonded sperm maintained normal motility and viability. This study may indicate that drug-using fathers may cause developmental abnormalities in offspring, if the cocaine is carried directly into the conceptus.